A VISITOR'S GUIDE TO VICTORIAN ENGLAND

Michelle Higgs

PEN & SWORD HISTORY

First published in 2014 by

an imprint of
Pen & Sword Books Ltd
47 Church Street
Barnsley
South Yorkshire
S70 2AS

ISBN:- 9781781592830

A CIP catalogue record for this book is
available from the British Library.

Printed and bound in the UK by CPI Group (UK) Ltd,
Croydon, CRO 4YY

Pen & Sword Books Ltd incorporates the imprints of Pen &
Sword Archaeology, Atlas, Aviation, Battleground, Discovery,
Family History, History, Maritime, Military, Naval, Politics,
Railways, Select, Social History, Transport, True Crime, and
Claymore Press, Frontline Books, Leo Cooper, Praetorian
Press, Remember When, Seaforth Publishing and Wharncliffe.

For a complete list of Pen & Sword titles please contact
PEN & SWORD BOOKS LIMITED
47 Church Street, Barnsley, South Yorkshire, S70 2AS, England
E-mail: enquiries@pen-and-sword.co.uk
Website: www.pen-and-sword.co.uk

A VISITOR'S GUIDE TO VICTORIAN ENGLAND

Michelle Higgs

Contents

Acknowledgements

While writing this book, I received help and advice on locating information and illustrations from a number of different sources.

For this assistance, I would like to express my gratitude to the staff of Cadbury Research Library: Special Collections, University of Birmingham; The Sainsbury Archive, Museum of London Docklands; Durham County Record Office; and to Paul Jarman of Beamish, The Living Museum of the North.

I would also like to thank Jackie Depelle, Jackie Reid and Sue Wilkes who were so generous with their time and their research, and my editor, Jen Newby for her thoughtful suggestions and attention to detail.

Finally, I would like to thank my husband Carl for his continued patience and support, and my family and friends for their encouragement during the writing of this book.

ILLUSTRATIONS

Introduction

'The parks, the churches, the gardens, the theatres, the markets, the people, the streets, the carriages, the bridges, the exhibitions, the fairs, the bazars [sic], the customs, the manners, all are full of interest, and keep one's senses and imagination continually upon the stretch; and yet I have scarcely begun to see what is to be seen.'
(Henry Colman, *European Life and Manners*, 1850)

This was the American author Henry Colman's reaction when he visited London for the first time, but it could apply to any place or decade in Victorian England. This book allows you to follow in his footsteps and explore this fascinating country yourself.

The Victorians were brilliant inventors of many things we take for granted today – cameras, telephones and bicycles to name a few – so prepare to be amazed! This handy guide will help you to survive in a very different era. It tells you almost everything you'll need to know during your trip, including the correct etiquette at a dinner party, how to use a bathing machine, and what to do if you fall ill. Certain items will help you to blend in and keep you safe, so don't forget to pack the following:

- A hat – everyone wears a hat, whether rich or poor, so to passers-by, you'll look positively naked without one.
- An umbrella – yes, the weather's still temperate, so

an umbrella will shelter you come rain or shine. It also makes a good, makeshift weapon if you need to protect yourself from pickpockets or unwanted attention, or if you inadvertently get into a fight.

• Lots of handkerchiefs – these are useful for covering your face when the noxious smells of sewage and slime get too strong; they're also handy for wiping dirt, mud and excrement from your shoes or hems.

• Insect powder – this kills bedbugs and fleas, ensuring you have a better chance of getting a good night's sleep; there's a strong possibility that you'll need it at your hotel or lodgings.

• Indigestion pills – these are indispensable after a heavy Victorian dinner of numerous courses, plus entrées and desserts, but they are often mild laxatives too, so be prepared!

Armed with these five essentials, you're ready to explore. Off you go…

Weave your way through the crowds at the market where you'll find well-dressed middle-class ladies and gentlemen in their finery, rubbing shoulders with the smart but shabbier working classes. The tantalising smell of hot coffee wafts from a stall on your left, which is percolating nicely with that of fresh, steaming horse manure just yards away on the cobbles. There are so many stalls that it's hard to take it all in. Gleaming tin pots and pans, live songbirds in cages, second-hand corsets: you can buy practically anything at the market.

Hundreds of shouting voices, shrill and deep, mingle together, trying to tempt customers to purchase their wares. "Turnips, a penny a bunch!", "Beautiful

Yarmouth bloaters, three a penny!" and "Who'll buy my chestnuts, a penny a score!". In the distance, the jaunty music of a barrel-organ starts, but it's drowned out by someone playing a tuba.

Out of the corner of your eye, you spot a young, shoeless urchin stealing a few red apples from a stall; he makes a run for it through the throng of shoppers and sellers. The wizened old woman who runs the stall protests loudly and in the hue and cry that follows, no-one notices when the moustachioed gentleman standing nearby has his pocket picked, relieving him of his green silk handkerchief and his money. Welcome to Victorian England, where you'll need your wits about you at all times…

Chapter One
Getting Your Bearings

'You will not have gone a hundred paces along the street with a valise or bag in your hand, without having a band of street boys and loafers at your heels. They are all on the look-out for a chance of earning a penny, if you confide your luggage to them to carry, or of disappearing round the corner with it, if you turn your back an instant. If you require to cross the road, a beggar in rags will step in front of you, and sweep away the mud out of your path with his broom. You will come across these poor devils in the most fashionable quarters.'
(Max O'Rell, *John Bull and His Island*, 1884)

Arriving on a busy Victorian street is a bewildering and intimidating experience, and an assault on the senses. There is a cacophony of noise: the lusty cries of street sellers like costermongers, muffin-men, and flower-girls; the clip-clop of horses' hooves on cobblestones and the jingle of their harnesses; the impromptu performances by dancers and street musicians with barrel-organs and hurdy-gurdies; and the voices of the crowds jostling for space along the half-made pavements and muddy streets churned up by horse-drawn vehicles.

'The noise of the street is at times overpowering to a person of weak nerves, and the confusion indescribable', wrote David W. Bartlett in *What I Saw in London* (1853). 'The policeman with his leather-topped hat and baton is busy giving an order here, assisting there, and exercising in a laughable manner his authority'.

In addition to the deafening din, a heady concoction of unpleasant odours emanates from every corner. The stench of horse manure, animal dung and human waste overflowing from cesspits and open sewers mingles with that of rotting fish, meat and vegetables; smoke and soot; and the general odour of unwashed people and rarely-laundered clothing. Add the offensive smells created by the leather tanning industry and slaughter houses wafting in from the outskirts, and you end up with an incredible stink. It can be unbearable, but you are still outside in the open air! Just wait until you enter a building…

What you will see, hear and smell will depend on whether you're visiting a vast city, large town or rural village. Wherever you are, watch your step because debris, rubbish and dung are everywhere. The underclass of scavengers collects every scrap of detritus but it's still possible to slip over on discarded peelings or oyster shells if you're not looking carefully.

You may be shocked to see 'pure-finders' picking up dog excrement in the street with their bare hands; they sell it on to leather-dressers and tanners. An American, John Henry Sherburne, who visited England in 1847, wrote that on passing through the great thoroughfares of Liverpool, 'the most disgusting sight' to him 'was seeing women and young girls employed in scraping up street manure with their naked hands, and placing it in baskets, or their aprons'. He concluded, 'These scenes are so common, as not to be noticed by the citizens'.

COME RAIN OR SHINE

The scene in the streets changes at different times of the year. In the sweltering heat of summer, clouds of dust created by horse-drawn vehicles settle on clothing, windows and faces, while piles of horse manure and dung attract swarms of flies. In her memoir *Period Piece*, Gwen Raverat recalled how in summer 'the thick white dust came powdering in at all the windows; rising in clouds from the horses' hooves, and whitening the grass and the trees across the road... And everywhere and all the time there was the smell of horses; it came in at the windows with the dust'.

At all times of the year, the sooty skies create a grimy atmosphere, especially in large towns and cities, spoiling clothing and furnishings alike. 'An Old Correspondent' from the country wrote to *The Magazine of Domestic Economy* in 1842, after visiting London for the season, complaining of the 'multitudinous blacks' that poured in at every open window; spoiling each article of wearing apparel which would have remained unharmed for years in the country'. She suggested to her hostess that she fit muslin blinds to the windows with the positive result that 'instead of finding on my toilet table showers of black snow, my sleeping apartment and dressing-room were always airy, and nearly as clean as the rooms of my home in the country'.

You can experience the legendary thick, acrid fogs of English cities, especially London, at any time of the year. They are so bad that breathing is often made difficult and visibility is extremely poor. When Reverend Francis Kilvert visited London in February 1873, there was 'a thick yellow fog all day. London very dark and it was of no use to go to see pictures. Candles at breakfast and needful till ten o'clock'.

The 'oozy, jammy mud' of Gwen Raverat's childhood frequently causes accidents when horses slip over in the middle of the street. The Victorians love a spectacle and you will see a crowd gathering whenever it happens. Miraculously, as quickly as the incident occurs, it is cleared away. There is always a good-natured driver who helps to unbuckle the harness, while another bystander calms the horse and keeps his head down.

There is a different hazard for horses during harsh winters as there are deep, frozen ruts made by the wheels of carts, carriages and omnibuses which scar the roads, rendering them dangerous and often impassable.

STREET ETIQUETTE

Although you will naturally be curious and want to linger to peer in the windows of drapers' shops, jewellers and fancy bazaars, this is not advisable on busy city streets. You will be pushed and jostled along by people going about their daily business, so don't be surprised if you have a few bruises by the end of the day.

George Frederick Pardon warns readers of *The Popular Guide to London and its Suburbs* (1852) to 'avoid lingering in crowded thoroughfares, and keep the right-hand to the wall'. He adds:

'Never enter into conversation with men who wish to show you the way, offer to sell 'smuggled cigars' or invite you to take a glass of ale or play a game at skittles. If in doubt about the direction of any street or building, inquire at a respectable shop, or of the nearest policeman. Do not relieve street-beggars and avoid byeways and poor neighbourhoods after dark. Carry no more money than is necessary for the day's expenses. Look after your watch and chain, and take care of your pockets at the entrance to theatres, exhibitions, churches, and in the omnibuses and streets.'

You would be a fool indeed if you walk about with your watch, purse or pocket-book (for holding banknotes) on show. There are pockets in a man's coat tails, but it is best not to put anything valuable there as they are easily picked. Gentlemen's watches are usually carried in waistcoat pockets, and a highly-skilled thief can even steal from here without the owner noticing. Ladies' pockets are deep in their dresses, but because of their multiple layers of petticoats or their crinolines, a pickpocket can easily put their whole hand in undetected and filch valuables hidden there.

Pickpockets have their own social hierarchy and crimes are often committed by organised gangs, each member playing their part. Henry Mayhew termed the pickpocket a 'mobsman' in *London Labour and the*

London Poor (1861). This criminal took his name from 'the gregarious habits of the class to which he belongs, it being necessary for the successful picking of pockets that the work be done in small gangs or mobs, so as to "cover" the operator'. The 'mobsman' 'usually dresses in the same elaborate style of fashion as a Jew on a Saturday… and "mixes" generally in the "best of company", frequenting for the purposes of business, all the places of public entertainment, and often being a regular attendant at church , and the more elegant chapels – especially during charity sermons'.

Executions of criminals took place in public until 1868 and they always drew large crowds, making them another favourite haunt of pickpockets. 'Buzzers' specialise in picking gentlemen's pockets, while 'wires' are more manually dextrous and can pick a lady's pocket with ease. The railway 'sneak' is another thief who will quickly walk off with your overcoat, cape or portmanteau if they are left unattended. Nine times out of ten, you won't realise you've become a victim to thieves until after the event, but if you do notice someone getting too close for comfort, you could always shout or scream for help, or threaten them with your trusty umbrella.

As you walk about, you'll notice that advertising is everywhere, from the omnibuses and railway carriages through to the walking sandwich-board men and the hundreds of handbills distributed every day by young boys. To stand out from the crowd, the advertisers have to be creative. In *Saunterings In and About London* (1853), Max Schlesinger recalls seeing 'three immense wooden pyramids advertising a new panorama of Egypt; a mosque publicising "a most marvellous Arabian medicine, warranted to cure the bite of mad dogs and venomous reptiles generally" and a trumpeting chariot inviting visitors to Vauxhall'.

CROSSING THE ROAD

If you try to cross a busy street at a spot other than a main crossing, you will seriously endanger your life. Horse-drawn vehicles of all descriptions are wedged in together so it is nigh on impossible to reach the other side of the road without injury. While you wait with the other pedestrians, make sure you have a penny ready to hand to the ragged crossing sweeper who keeps the area clear of mud and dung. If you do not pay him, he may not be so courteous next time.

You'll find that some areas of the road are paved with wooden blocks, rather than cobblestones. This is to deaden the thundering noise of the traffic and also to spare the horses, since there is less chance of them slipping on wood. However, it is difficult to maintain and from the 1870s onwards, it's more common to see roads which have been macadamised or resurfaced with asphalt.

AFTER DARK

When night falls, the hiss of the gas-lights becomes a part of the city soundscape. They are lit each evening by a man with a ladder and a hand-lamp, who also extinguishes the lamps on his round the next morning. The streets take on a cheerier feel as even the smallest shops are illuminated. From butchers to bakers, gin palaces to markets, all burn gas from one-inch tubes to attract evening customers. You'll find that opening hours are far longer on Saturdays than on any other night of the week. This is when the working classes have been paid and still have money to spend.

One rung below them on the social ladder, the poverty-stricken live in the miserable squalor of narrow alleys and courtyards, cheek by jowl with the wealthy. On a visit to Liverpool in 1839, Lord Shaftesbury 'surveyed the town, admired its buildings, commended its broad streets, and wondered at its wealth'. He then saw 'thousands of the dirtiest, worst-clad children…presenting a strange inconsistency with the signs of luxury all around'. One peep into the side-alleys revealed they had come from the Irish immigrant quarter, where some of the most deprived people in English cities lived.

Middle-class observers (also known as 'slummers'), who visited the poorest districts of urban England, all reported on the vast numbers of children about the streets. 'At one time, in a narrow alley, I had fourteen or fifteen all round me, dirty, barefoot, one tiny girl carrying an infant, a baby still at breast but whose whitish head was completely bald', wrote Hippolyte Taine in *Notes on England* (1872). 'Nothing could be more dismal than these livid little bodies, the pale, stringy hair, the cheeks of flabby flesh encrusted with old filth. They kept running up, pointing out the "gentleman" to each other with curious and avid gestures'.

DOWN IN THE COUNTRY

Anyone visiting a large English city from the countryside will experience the same bewilderment that you feel as a visitor from modern times. The pace of life, the numbers of people, the volume of traffic, and the level of noise are all markedly different in rural areas.

Contrasting London with a visit to Surrey, David W. Bartlett wrote:

> 'Hamlets, hedges, farm-houses and cottage-homes were scattered at our feet. The village green was below in full view, and out upon it were boys and girls shouting for very happiness...Around the farm-houses the quiet cows were gathered, and the milkmaids were at their work...every garden bloomed with choice flowers... No rude noise startled us; the music of a tiny stream touched our ears pleasantly; there were no harsh London noises; no dismal sights and noxious scents; no whining mendicants or flaunting prostitutes'.

As long as you are dressed correctly in Victorian attire, you can blend in easily with an urban crowd. This is not the case in a small country village where strangers are a novelty. At first, the number of stares you will attract may make you think there is something amiss with your appearance but it is simply that in village life, everyone knows everyone else.

The pretty rural Cheshire village of Davenham in the late nineteenth century was recalled by a contributor to Pat Barr's *I Remember*:

*'the shops supplied almost all our wants. The public
bake houses baked for the people who made their own
bread, the butcher killed his own meat, also he killed the
pigs for the cottagers, for almost every cottage had a sty
and kept a pig. The shoe-shop sold, made and mended
boots and shoes…There were two tailor shops, who made
everybody's suits and the corn miller and the saddler,
also a livery stables, which had cabs and a wagonette
for hire. There were also the painters and plumbers, a
small builders and repairers…Davenham was fortunate
in having so many craftsmen of one kind and another'.*

It is on market days when quiet country towns really
come alive, as described by Richard Jefferies in *Hodge
and His Masters* (1880): 'Cart-horses furbished up
for sale, with strawbound tails and glistening skins;
baaing flocks of sheep; squeaking pigs; bullocks with
their heads held ominously low…; lads rushing hither
and thither; dogs barking; everything and everybody
crushing, jostling, rushing through the narrow street'.

WHAT TO LOOK OUT FOR

Whether you're visiting a great city, a sleepy market
town or a rural village, it's important to get your bearings
before you start exploring. Start by identifying prominent
landmarks, such as the railway station in large towns and
cities or, in more rural areas, the local inn. You could also
try using a local map created especially for tourists, one
of the by-products of railway development, which can be
bought at booksellers and stationers.

As a stranger, you should think of the police officers clad in blue (nicknamed 'bluebottles') as your new best friends. In towns, you can always turn to them if you are lost or you have been the victim of a crime. When he visited Liverpool in 1847, John Henry Sherburne found the police to be numerous and present in every square. In *The Tourist's Guide*, he wrote, 'Their regulations are most admirable, and their polite attention to strangers, both day and night, is proverbial; going frequently much out of their way to serve them, and are never known to take the smallest fee for their trouble'.

Walking around the streets, it may appear that Victorian England is an exclusively male-oriented world. Until the 1870s, unaccompanied females in the streets of towns and cities were presumed to be prostitutes so they were a no-go area for the respectable. Gradually, the look of the streets changes over time, as it becomes more common to see unmarried women and girls shopping or eating out, using omnibuses and trains to get to work, or taking part in the craze for cycling.

As one Englishman, who had been abroad for 30 years, put it, 'Girls of every rank think no more of riding a bicycle through the busy thoroughfares of London, than they do of going into an A.B.C. shop for a cup of tea. Go back to 1875, and try to think, if you can, what would have been said of a woman riding a bicycle down Piccadilly on a June afternoon'.

Don't forget, if you lose your way, you can always ask for help in a post office or a respectable-looking shop. These retailers and the police can all provide recommendations for decent, comfortable accommodation, which should mean that you avoid the seediest lodgings.

Chapter Two
Accommodation

'We are staying at the Imperial Burdon Hotel, expensive, but very comfortable, old-fashioned and clean, quiet, a civil waiter 'if you please, sir', and good cooking. The Burdon Hotel we found most excellent, but extortionate, £20.9.0 for one week, three persons, a sitting room but no table d'hôte. This decided us not to stay the fortnight, so we moved to Salisbury.'

(Beatrix Potter, diary entry, 1895)

The English hotel is essentially a by-product of the railways; before train travel was possible, the main places to stay were rustic hostelries and inns. Recognising the need to provide comfortable accommodation for their customers, the railway companies built top-class hotels next to the stations. Foreign visitors found the accommodation at Charing Cross, St Pancras and Paddington (the Great Western Royal) particularly impressive. The best hotels offered sumptuous public rooms, as well as comfort and luxury in the bedrooms.

According to *The Midland Railway* (1888), the Grand Hotel at the St Pancras railway terminus in London is 'regarded as unsurpassed and perhaps unequalled for combined comfort and magnificence in Europe'. It has a general coffee room on the ground floor which sweeps along the whole curved wing of the building. If you walk up the grand staircase, you will reach the first floor where there is a general reading and drawing room, a music room, and a private coffee room. Continuing along the deep-piled silent Axminster carpet, there are suites of rooms with balconies overlooking the Euston Road.

The guide continues: 'The spacious and lofty apartments, the handsome furniture, the Brussels carpets, the massive silken or woollen curtains, and the pinoleum blinds; the wardrobes, chests of drawers, clocks, writing tables, sofas, arm-chairs, with which they are supplied, leave nothing to be desired by the wealthiest and the most refined'. On the upper floors, there are three to four hundred other bedrooms, of various sizes.

If you want to experience a stay in a Victorian hotel, you'll need lots of spare cash. They are notoriously expensive but the cost of a room can be cut, if you're fit enough to climb lots of stairs and you don't mind having a view of a blank wall or a stable-yard.

The largest and most expensive hotels do not necessarily provide the best experience for visitors because they can still offer 'bad cooking, wretched beds, and miserable attendance' for an exorbitant price, according to Lillias Campbell Davidson in *Hints to Lady Travellers*. Bear in mind that most hotels and other accommodation providers charge for extras. In 1852, a writer to *The Times* complained about being charged by a hotel the rate of 2s 6d per day for 2½d worth of coals!

When London fund-holder William Aldous married his second wife Sophia in 1862, they honeymooned for a week in Malvern, staying at the Link Hotel. Their final bill came to £13 4s 6d for the period of 3 to 11 October, with an extra fee for the chambermaid 'for her attention'. The bill would have included the accommodation and all meals, plus extras such as bottles of sherry and coals. The high cost indicates that the couple may have stayed in a superior room, or perhaps a suite.

On 11 October, William wrote in his diary: 'Good accommodation at Mitre Oxford and at the Link Hotel Malvern, little if anything to find fault with, thankful for having retd. in safety and for all the blessings allowed us'. The couple's first-class train tickets from Malvern to London were £2 6s, but William paid a further £2 6s 6d to the porter at Worcester, where they had to change trains. (*Diary of William Aldous 1862-1864 MS 133/1, reproduced by permission of Cadbury Research Library: Special Collections, University of Birmingham.*)

As with all other forms of accommodation, it's best to find a hotel through personal recommendation, for instance, at the local Post Office or from the station-master at the railway station. You could also consult a tourist guide for an impartial view of local amenities. For example, in 1841 at Crosby, Waterloo, guide-writer Augustus Bozzi Granville inspected the beds and sitting rooms of the Waterloo Hotel:

'For two pounds sixteen shillings a week, a single person may board and lodge at this house, which in every way resembles some of the best appointed hotels at other and more fashionable sea-bathing places. The coffee-room is airy and neatly appointed; the bedrooms are of moderate size, and all those on the second floor overlook the sands, and are consequently preferred. Everything in the house looks clean, including the landlady'.

19

A penny for the 'boots'

You will need to keep some money aside as gratuities for the servants, including the chambermaid, the 'boots' and the waiter. They usually do not receive proper wages and depend almost entirely on the generosity of visitors. The amount for tips is rarely added to the final bill, so you will have to pay the servants yourself and gauge how much is appropriate; this is particularly the case up to the 1870s.

Deciding how much to tip can be perplexing. *Black's Picturesque Tourist and Road and Railway Guide Book Through England and Wales* (1850) helpfully provides a suggested scale. If you're a single gentleman taking one or two meals as a passing traveller, 6d each for the waiter, chambermaid and porter (or 'boots') is sufficient. If you're staying a day and a night and taking meals in the hotel, the guide suggests 1s 6d or 2s for the servants, and if staying several days, 1s or 1s 6d per day.

The fact that single women are not mentioned proves that lone female travellers in Victorian times are a rare breed. The guide goes on to point out 'in country and village inns, even the lowest of the payments…may be unnecessarily liberal, while in some of the fashionable hotels in London, the highest may be considerably under par'.

On his first visit to England in 1847, the American John Henry Sherburne stayed at the Black Bear in Manchester, but he was unaware that service was not included. He paid his moderate bill and while getting into his cab, he was 'surrounded by all the servants of the establishment, asking to be remembered from the head cook to the boots'. He was later advised by a friend that, when asking for his bill at a hotel, he should insist that the servants also be charged in it. In this way, he would find himself 'a few pounds the richer' and save himself 'much trouble and mortification'.

The English system of fees 'has its good side, and I never travel without finding the advantage of it, especially on railways, where the officials are strictly forbidden to take fees, and where, in consequence, a fee secures twice as much good service as anywhere else', wrote Nathaniel Hawthorne in his *English Note-Books* (1871). 'Be it recorded, that I never knew an Englishman refuse a shilling – or for that matter, a halfpenny'.

RUSTIC INNS

In small market towns or country districts off the beaten track, the best option for strangers is to find accommodation at a respectable-looking inn. These are often advertised in the local Post Office directory or gazetteer. For example, an advertisement for the Reindeer Inn, in Mill Street, Kidderminster, appears in the 1873 *Gazetteer and Directory of Worcestershire*. The inn is run by Henry Hill and he offers 'superior wines and spirits' as well as 'good accommodation for commercial travellers'.

A country inn can be infinitely more pleasurable to stay in than a large hotel. Nathaniel Hawthorne describes the Swan Hotel at Newby Bridge as 'an old-fashioned inn, where the landlord and his people have a simple and friendly way of dealing with guests, and yet provide them with all sorts of facilities for being comfortable. They load our supper and breakfast tables with trout, cold beef, ham, toast and muffins; and give us three fair courses of dinner, and excellent wine'.

FURNISHED APARTMENTS

For a stay of longer than a couple of nights, furnished apartments are less expensive than a hotel and often considered preferable to accommodation offered by a boarding-house. When viewing apartments, it's advisable to personally inspect each room to check their cleanliness. Once you move in, keep all valuables locked away as a precaution. 'Landladies may be perfectly honest, and should always be considered so till they prove themselves unworthy of the trust; so may their servants but...[they] are drawn from a very inferior class, and it is neither right nor kind to expose them to temptation which they may be unable to resist', comments Lillias Campbell Davidson.

As with hotels, you will be charged for 'extras' in addition to the fee for the apartments. These include fires in the kitchen at all seasons, and other fires you have ordered; lights; cleaning boots; washing bed and table linen; use of the cruet stand; and attendance.

The American author, Henry Colman, visited England in 1843. In *European Life,* he describes how when he first arrived in London, he stayed at a hotel for five days, and then sought private lodgings. He found 'one of the best places in the town for its central and convenient situation, and for its airiness and quiet, and...for its neatness and comfort'. He had a parlour and bedroom, 'neatly and handsomely furnished' for 30 shillings a week. The price covered breakfast and tea, at whatever time he wanted, and dinner 'if I choose, charging me the cost of the articles'. Extras included fire and candles (at cost), one shilling for cleaning boots and errands, and tips for the chambermaid. He could have rented apartments at 20 shillings a week, but they were situated over the river and not as convenient. The family who kept the lodgings were tradespeople but 'keep my rooms in the best possible order, and do every thing they can for my comfort'.

Bachelor lodgings are different from 'family lodgings' as they offer fewer rooms, perhaps a sitting-room, bedroom and dressing-room, and sometimes only a bedroom. 'According to English ideas, the worst room in the house is too good for a bachelor', wrote Max Schlesinger. 'What does a bachelor care for a three-legged chair, a broken window, a ricketty [sic] table, and a couple or so of sportive currents? It is exactly as if a man took a special delight in rheumatism, tooth-ache, hard beds, smoking chimneys, and the society of rats until he has entered the holy state of matrimony'.

The main disadvantage of furnished apartments is that meals are not normally provided for you, unless you have made a special arrangement with the landlady. Nor do you have any means of making even a cup of tea, until you have placed orders with the local tradesmen.

BOARDING-HOUSES

If you stay in a boarding-house, you will find out a great deal about the Victorians. Meals will be provided, served for all the boarders together around one large table, and you will join in with them. You'll need to bring your own beer or wine as boarding-houses are not licensed to sell alcohol. If the landlady is mean with her portion sizes, the other boarders may undertake some illicit cooking in their bedrooms, such as toasting bread in front of their fires.

At a boarding-house, 'one is cast from morning till night into a sort of spurious family circle composed of total strangers, among whom there will doubtless be always a pleasant element, but amongst whom, as in all gatherings of poor human nature, there are sure to be uncongenial or offensive people', writes Lillias Campbell Davidson. Your bedroom is the only place where you will be able to get any privacy, as the small sitting-room is shared with everyone else. This makes it difficult to avoid talking to boring or insufferable people, but you will quickly become the subject of gossip if you remain too aloof. Heated arguments often occur when people holding opposite views are staying in the house.

If you are male and single, it may be best to pretend you are married. According to *The Graphic* (1890), in a boarding-house there is sometimes 'a great scarcity of men (on one occasion the proportion was 7 to 1), the one being in great demand until it was discovered he was married'.

Many boarding-houses specialise in accommodation for commercial travellers, while others try to attract gentlemen and their families. An advertisement for Mount Pleasant, Great Malvern in the *Gazetteer and Directory of Worcestershire* (1873) claims it is a 'first-class' boarding and lodging house run by Mrs Mary Ann Burlingham. The house is situated in the very centre of Malvern close to the Abbey Church, Post Office, and gentlemen's club. The rooms are 'lofty and spacious, and are fitted up in the most convenient and liberal style, for the accommodation of Gentlemen and Families of position'.

LODGING HOUSES

If you're very short of money, the cheapest accommodation can be found in a lodging house. These are divided into 'better class' establishments and 'common' or 'low' lodging houses, where the price for a bed is as low as three pence per night. Even in the more respectable accommodation, don't be surprised if you are offered a bed shared with a stranger, especially if you are male; this was a very common practice.

In 1859, while visiting Birmingham to see a medical consultant, William Fletcher engaged a bed at Suffield's in Union Passage but discovered there were bedbugs in the room: 'I was removed into another room – a double bedded one, where I surprised some old fogy, who had just woke up. There I met with another nuisance. The old bloke snored to that degree that he must have been heard in the street – worse than ½ doz pigs I can safely say. I couldn't suppress a laugh at the predicament I was in'.

If you stay in a better class of lodging house, spare a thought for the poor maid-of-all-work who has to attend every bell at all hours of the day with very little respite or time off. Give her any spare change you have as she is wretchedly paid by her mistress.

You won't find a 'common' or 'low' lodging house in the Post Office directory or tourist guide. They are the haunts of 'beggars, thieves and prostitutes, and those in training for thieves and prostitutes – the exceptions are those who must lodge at the lowest possible cost. Fights, and fierce fights too, are common in them', according to an inmate interviewed by Henry Mayhew in *London Labour and the London Poor* (1861). If you dare to venture into one of these establishments, you will have to pay as soon as you get there or be turned out onto the street. Inside, you'll find the beds are nothing more than straw or rags, and huge numbers of adults and children are squashed into small, unventilated rooms.

The same inmate shared his experience of 'low' lodging houses with Mayhew:

> *'Nothing can be worse to the health than these places; without ventilation, cleanliness or decency, and with forty people's breaths, perhaps, mingling together in one foul choking steam of stench...There is a pair of sheets, a blanket and a rug. I have known the bedding to be unchanged for three months; but that is not general. The beds are an average size. Dirt is the rule with them, and cleanliness the exception. They are all infested with vermin; I never met with an exception...A pail in the middle of a room, to which both sexes may resort, is a frequent arrangement.'*

You will probably find yourself scratching almost straight away. One City missionary reported, 'The quantities of vermin are amazing. I have entered a room, and in a few minutes I have felt them dropping on my hat from the ceiling like peas'. Another inmate confessed: 'I have been so tormented with the itch, that on two occasions I filled my pockets with stones, waited till a policeman came up and then broke a lamp, that I might be sent to prison, and there be cleansed, as is required before newcomers are admitted'.

Staying in a 'low' lodging house is undoubtedly detrimental to your health and you should only turn to one as a last resort.

STAYING WITH A FAMILY

You will discover far more about the lives of ordinary people by living like a local. Of all the classes of Victorian society, you are most likely to be offered a bed by a middle-class acquaintance. For the middle classes, appearances are everything and you may find that your new friend puts on airs and graces to impress you. As a visitor, you will probably only see the drawing room (the most lavishly decorated room in the house), the dining room and your own bedroom. In the middle-class home, the drawing room is where the 'best' and most formal furniture and furnishings are placed. The middle classes lap up the advice of authors like Mrs Jane Panton in *From Kitchen to Garret* (1888), in which she offers suggestions for furnishing the home to indicate the status of the householder.

The middle-class drawing room is where guests are received and entertained, and is otherwise rarely used. This is despite Mrs Panton's assertion that 'it is quite useless to attempt to have a pretty drawing-room, unless the owner really means to have it in constant use, and intends to sit in it regularly. I am quite convinced that rooms resent neglect just as human beings do, and that they become morose and sulky-looking if they are kept closed, or only opened when strangers are expected'.

If you're invited to dinner in a middle-class home, it's

highly likely that their lone overworked servant will be asked to cook something special, perhaps from a menu suggested in Mrs Beeton's popular *Book of Household Management* (1861). These dinners generally consist of three courses, plus entrées and desserts.

If you're lucky enough to be invited to stay in a wealthy upper-class household, you would be well advised to read an etiquette guide before you go. Moving in polite society according to the rules of propriety is a minefield, and a great deal can go wrong! At an upper-class house, you'll notice an army of servants on hand to cater to your every whim. You will be expected to dress formally for dinner; try not to be overwhelmed by the number of courses served and the sheer wealth on display in terms of sumptuous furnishings. *Cassell's Handbook of Etiquette* (1860) advises dinner party guests to 'use your fork and spoon for pies and puddings, in preference to your knife' and to use 'silver-bladed knives' with your fruit, except with small fruit when only a spoon is required.

The guide also stresses that you should not 'help yourself to a dish without knowing the nature of it'. This is because if you dislike it and send it away, 'you might impress the other guests with the idea that it was not good of its kind'. Finger-glasses of warm water, with doyleys on plates, are brought in with the dessert. Simply dip your fingers in the glasses and wipe them with your dinner napkin or doyley, but 'abstain from the disgusting practice of publicly rinsing your mouth. It is to be hoped that you performed all the duties of your toilette before you joined the company'.

After dinner, if you're male, you will go with the other gentlemen to the smoking room, while if you're female, you'll accompany the ladies to the drawing room for coffee and conversation. Unlike the middle-class household, there will be a distinct absence of children as they will be kept well out of sight (and earshot) in the separate nursery wing. On leaving, remember to tip the footman.

At the other end of the social scale, don't assume that all working-class households are overcrowded and insanitary; you may be surprised by the comforts in the homes of those in regular employment or where their children are contributing to the family's income. In the parlour (which is kept for 'best'), there is often 'a piano with a fretwork front and a pleated silk back,' recalled a Lancashire contributor to Pat Barr's *I Remember*:

> *'In the middle of the room is a table with a plush cloth on it and the Family Bible in the middle and, as it is a weekday, stocking legs cover the table legs. Opposite the fireplace there is a 'dresser' with lustres at each end…On the wall above is a long cased clock…Under the window [is] a couch with a woollen cushion at each end and an antimacassar on the back. In the window a pair of lace curtains, a paper blind, an aspidistra and a fern plant on the window sill'.*

Living conditions are not always bad even when a family has to eat, sleep and live in one room. You may be lucky enough to find a household like that of the struggling costermonger Henry Mayhew met in London. He lived in a front kitchen and there were five in the family, including his mother-in-law, but only one bed. Although they were, in effect, living in a cellar, 'there was the usual attempt to make the fireside comfortable. The stone sides had been well whitened, and the mantel-piece decorated with its small tin trays, tumblers and a piece of looking-glass. A cat with a kitten were seated on the hearthrug in front...Over the head, on a string that stretched from wall to wall, dangled a couple of newly-washed shirts... Every endeavour had been made to give the home a look of comfort. The window, with its paper-patched panes, had a clean calico blind [and] the side table was dressed up with yellow jugs and cups and saucers'.

By contrast, people without regular employment or those forced out of work by illness have very little money for rent, so they can only afford to live in the worst slums. For them, there are few improvements in housing by the end of the nineteenth century. In a series of reports entitled 'Scenes in Slumland', the *Birmingham Daily Gazette* (1901) described the quarters of the city's poorest inhabitants:

> *'Look at the begrimed windows, the broken glass, the apertures stopped with yellow paper or filthy rags; glance in at the rooms where large families eat and sleep every day and every night, amid rags and vermin, within dank and mildewed walls from which the blistered paper is drooping, or the bit of discoloration called 'paint' is peeling away. Here you can veritably taste the pestilential air, stagnant and mephitic.'*

In the countryside, the homes of the desperately poor also vary considerably in quality. While many people live in one-room hovels better suited as pig stys, others experience accommodation of a much higher standard. When Richard Heath visited northern England in 1893, he found living conditions there better than those in the south, even during the winter. In one cottage, 'The mahogany furniture, bright with hand-polish, the display of crockery and ornaments, the easy comfort of every arrangement, seen in the dancing light of a brilliant coal-fire, all tell of good housewifery and ample incomes. Every fireplace, too, has its set-pot and oven, being in constant requisition, for they have plenty of meat. Yet the good wife will tell you that they had a 'sair' fight for it before the children earned anything…On a winter's evening the family circle gather round the cheerful fire, the women knitting, the father mending shoes – an art nearly all acquire – while one of the younger ones reads for the benefit of the whole group'.

This may appear to paint a picture of a rural idyll, but country cottages are not always so welcoming. Richard Heath describes thatched mud cottages in Dorset as having 'no grate, but a huge open chimney… on which the miserable inhabitants place their fuel – sometimes nothing but clods of peat, emitting wretched acrid vapours'.

Owing to the low open chimneys, the houses are 'constantly filled with smoke, rendering the ceilings, where they have them, black and dingy enough. Around these wretched hearths the poor family crowd on a winter's night, stretching out their chilled hands and feet to gather what warmth they may. But some are so poverty-stricken that they can only afford to light a fire at meal-times; often their wet clothes can never be dried, but are put on damp again the next morning; for fuel is very expensive'.

AVOIDING VERMIN

As a visitor to Victorian England, you will very quickly discover the bane of nineteenth-century travellers (and homes): the bedbug. Variously known as wall-lice, 'B flats', punies or simply 'bugs', common bedbugs are blood-sucking parasites which feed mostly at night on the blood of humans. You will usually not know you have been bitten until you see red welts or blisters on your skin. The insects hide behind wallpaper, on the ceiling, in the crevices of bedsteads or on the bedding itself until they need to feed. Bedbugs can be unwittingly brought into a building in a traveller's trunk or servant's box, on someone's clothing or even with the freshly-returned laundry.

Placing the bedposts in cans of coal oil or paraffin is one way of preventing bedbugs from climbing up the bed, as is pulling the bed and furniture away from the walls by about two inches. Mercury chloride, otherwise known as 'bedbug poison', is effective but extremely toxic to humans. You can also buy pungent sulphur candles which produce sulphur dioxide when burned and kill bedbugs.

Using a pyrethrum-based insecticide powder (sometimes known as Persian powder), made from the root and leaves of chrysanthemums, is a safer method of eradicating bedbugs. One major brand of Victorian insect powder was Keating's. An advertisement dated 1887 advised that: 'A small quantity placed in the crevices of a bedstead will destroy bugs; a little sprinkled upon the pillow and sheets at bedtime will prevent persons being bitten by these and other offensive insects'. The powder is harmless to animals but 'unrivalled in destroying fleas, bugs, beetles, cockroaches & moths'. Keating's Powder is sold in tins at 6d, 1s and 2s 6d, so it is not affordable for the very poor. A cheaper alternative is Bayly's 'far-famed' insect killer, manufactured in Birmingham and sold by all chemists for one penny per packet.

Bed-bugs are said to smell like rotting raspberries. When Beatrix Potter stayed at the Osborne Hotel in Torquay in 1893, she wrote in her journal: 'I sniffed my bedroom on arrival, and for a few hours felt a certain grim satisfaction when my forebodings were maintained, but it is possible to have too much Natural History in a bed. I did not undress after the first night, but I was obliged to lie on it because there were only two chairs and one of them was broken. It is very uncomfortable to sleep with Keating's powder in the hair'.

Insect powder can also be used to kill the more dangerous insects commonly found in nineteenth-century homes, public transport and accommodation which include ticks, lice and fleas; these all carry diseases such as typhus and relapsing fever. Although bedbugs are a considerable nuisance, unless you have an allergic reaction to the bites, they will do you little harm.

With the general improvements in hygiene and sanitation in the final quarter of the nineteenth century, accommodation tends to be cleaner and more comfortable in this period, but standards still vary considerably. You'll also see far more English tourists from the 1870s onwards, taking advantage of the new Bank Holidays and the cheapness of railway excursions to visit the seaside and other beauty spots, as well as travellers from rural areas sightseeing in the capital for the first time.

Once you're settled into your accommodation, it's time to make sure you look the part with appropriate clothing so that you can easily pass unnoticed through a Victorian crowd.

Chapter Three
Clothing

'Except for the most small-waisted, naturally dumb-bell-shaped females, the ladies never seemed at ease, or even quite as if they were wearing their own clothes. For their dresses were always made too tight, and the bodices wrinkled laterally from the strain; and their stays showed in a sharp ledge across the middles of their backs. And in spite of whalebone, they were apt to bulge below the waist in front; for, poor dears, they were but human after all, and they had to expand somewhere.'
(Gwen Raverat, *Period Piece: A Cambridge Childhood*, 1952)

When you first arrive in Victorian England, it may appear that everyone is wearing the same kind of formal, tailored clothing, whether they are rich or poor. Even the urchins sport waistcoats and caps. This is half-true, but take a closer look when you're walking along the street, being served in a shop or waiting at a railway station. You'll soon spot the difference because nothing marks out the social class of a man or woman more than the quality of the clothes they wear. For children, particularly, the giveaway is the lack of shoes.

Nevertheless, the distinction between social classes can be blurred by clothing; people often wear finer clothes than perhaps they can afford to make a better impression. For instance, high-class courtesans and prostitutes wear fashionable, well-tailored clothing and domestic servants are often accused by their middle-class mistresses of dressing above their station, with cheap jewellery and flowers in their bonnets. Successful pickpockets can get close to their targets because they are well-dressed and merge easily with the middle and, sometimes, upper classes. A respectable-looking lady in elegant dress sitting in an omnibus may appear to have her hands neatly clasped on her lap, but they could be false and she may actually be a 'lady wire' with her real hands busy picking the pockets of the passengers next to her.

Hippolyte Taine vividly describes the recycling of Victorian clothing in *Notes on England* (1872):

'The climate is very dirty, things have to be changed and replaced frequently. Every newspaper carries the advertisements of dealers who will come to your house and buy your part-worn clothes. Immaculate appearance is obligatory for a gentleman: his suits, once past their best, go to a man of the lower classes and end up in rags on the back of a pauper. Hence one's clothes are a badge of social rank. In nothing is the distance between classes so clearly indicated as in a man's appearance. Imagine a dandy's evening suit, or a lady's pink, flowered hat: the one you will see again on some poor wretch huddled on the steps leading down to the Thames, the other at Shadwell on the head of an old hag sorting rags and rubbish. Imagine what a lady's hat can become after having passed for three or four years from one head to another, been dented against walls, bashed in by blows.'

In the Victorian period, the sober look of men's clothing is in extreme contrast to the brightly-coloured and decorative clothes of women. 'Both sexes, but more particularly women, looked like the sturdily upholstered furniture which could be seen in Victorian homes, well padded, richly covered and extravagantly trimmed', writes Valerie Cumming in *Exploring Costume History*. You'll also be astonished by the sheer number of layers of underclothing people wear, especially women, and the weight of all this material. The underclothing of many ladies weighed up to 14 pounds and the Rational Dress Society campaigned from the 1880s for a limit of seven pounds in weight.

In the late nineteenth century, Gwen Raverat shared a room with another young lady for a night. In *Period Piece*, she recalls the layers of underclothes that her friend wore: 'Thick, long-legged, long-sleeved woollen combinations; over them, white cotton combinations, with plenty of buttons and frills; very serious, bony, grey stays, with suspenders; black woollen stockings; white cotton drawers, with buttons and frills; white cotton 'petticoat-bodice', with embroidery, buttons and frills; rather short, white flannel petticoat; [and a] long alpaca petticoat, with a flounce round the bottom'.

Working-class people wear fewer layers of clothing. Their garments have to be practical enough for doing manual work; for instance, tight corsets are not worn by servants simply because they need to bend down! By dressing in middle-class attire, it will be easy for you to blend in with the crowd without attracting too much attention. In essence, this social group wears less elaborate clothing than the upper classes, but still likes to look fashionable. Whatever you do, don't forget your hat.

WHAT TO WEAR: MEN

A shirt and a pair of drawers will form the basis of your underclothing. Drawers come in both long and short versions, but are always close-fitting on the legs. They open at the front and also have holes for the attachment of braces. From the 1880s, 'combinations', in the form of a vest and drawers crafted from one piece of fabric in natural wool, became very popular. The German Dr Gustav Jaeger invented these for health reasons, but they were quickly adopted for warmth. You may be very thankful to Dr Jaeger if you visit Victorian England in cold weather!

A man's shirt is an important indicator of his wealth and social status. Decorative detailing, a high fabric quality and clean, white cuffs all reveal that the wearer is not a manual worker. If you visit in the last quarter of the nineteenth century, you'll notice that over time, this distinction does change. The introduction of coloured shirts, detachable cuffs which can be reversed when soiled, and even 'cuff protectors' for office workers allows working men to keep themselves looking clean. Dress shirts for evening wear are always more extravagant and frilled than those for day wear. Collars are detachable from the shirt, and most men wear starched versions, which may be very uncomfortable at first. If you find these too difficult to wear, you could try some of the more informal turned-down collars worn from the 1860s onwards.

To the modern eye, the rest of your outfit is simply a formal suit. In the 1850s, men wear dress coats but by the 1860s, although they are still worn in the evenings, they are replaced by the frock coat for formal day wear. Twenty years later, the morning coat is in vogue. If you prefer a more informal style of dress, three-piece suits are popular from the late 1860s for the daytime, especially for sport, country and seaside wear. In tweed, check or plaid, they comprise matching waistcoats and trousers with a lounge jacket. In tailors' and outfitters' shops, you may also see the Norfolk jacket for sporting activities and the velvet or plush smoking jacket with a brightly-coloured lining.

You can add colour to your outfit by choosing a highly-patterned or vividly-toned waistcoat. However, from the 1870s, high-buttoned coats are fashionable and the waistcoat is no longer visible. Cravats and neckties, together with cufflinks and gold watch chains are also important elements of a man's wardrobe. Four-in-hand and Ascot are popular knots for neckties. Until the late 1880s and early 1890s, you will look distinctly out of place in Victorian England if you are clean-shaven. Moustaches, side-whiskers and beards are diligently cultivated, and whiskers are nicknamed 'mutton chops', 'Dundrearys' or 'Piccadilly weepers'. Fashionable men often scent their hair with perfumed Rowland's Macassar oil, which also purports to render their locks 'delightfully soft, silky, curly and glossy'. In the second half of the nineteenth century, this hair product is also marketed at women and children.

For middle-class men, good clothing was important since it helped them to look the part. John Whaley was an agent for a colliery in Allenhead, Northumbria. His house was in a village, and he had a position of some standing in the community. As a result, instead of having to go into town to order clothes, he was visited at home by the local tailor (for his own garments) and the draper (for his wife's clothing). On 22 March 1848, he wrote in his diary: 'George Short [tailor] called about Dinner time at our House. I ordered two Waistcoats, a Hat, a Cravat & a pair of Gloves of him'. Another diary entry from 27 April 1848 reads: 'John Barr [draper] called, we look'd through his Patterns and I ordered Doro' [his wife Dorothy] a new Black silk dress and some Articles for Fanny [his young daughter] & myself'.

Whaley also recorded some of the garments he had bought that year. They were clearly of varying quality, as some are described as 'good', while others are just 'middling', like one light vest, purchased from Richardsons as 'middling' and 'worn'. In March 1848, John Whaley bought no less than four different vests [waistcoats]: one in black silk velvet, another in red 'waved with silk', a third described as 'striped light' and one which was 'very light flowered'. Other items of clothing mentioned for 1848 include 'trowsers' in black cloth, dark grey and check; jackets specifically for the office; 'linnen' shirts and fronts; breasted and non-breasted cravats; and a coloured 'comforter', which was a woollen scarf. *(Diary entries reproduced by permission of Durham County Record Office: reference Durham County Record Office D/AR 65.)*

WHAT TO WEAR: WOMEN

As a woman visiting Victorian England, you'll quickly discover that dressing and undressing takes a considerable amount of time because of the sheer number of pieces of clothing which make up each outfit. Underneath your dress is a short-sleeved knee-length chemise and a pair of drawers with a corset on top. This is followed by either a stiffened horsehair petticoat, crinoline or bustle (depending on when you visit) to support the shape of your skirt, with one or two fabric petticoats worn over it. Fewer petticoats are needed when wearing a crinoline to create the same 'bell' effect.

Corsets (also known as 'stays') are heavily-boned, and can be laced tighter to create a smaller waistline. Even in the 1890s, 'it was a girl's ambition to have, at marriage, a waist-measurement not exceeding the number of years of her age – and to marry before she was 21', according to C. Willett and Phyllis Cunnington in *The History of Underclothes*. Unfortunately, achieving this ideal through tight lacing is detrimental to a woman's health as it compresses and deforms the ribs and liver – you have been warned!

The Magazine of Domestic Economy (1839) quotes the example of:

'a young lady...who prided herself upon possessing the smallest waist in the populous town of T_____, married, with every symptom of a speedy termination to her wedded life. She could not inhale a deep breath, her complexion had become thick, sallow, and liable

to cutaneous eruptions; she became more and more a martyr to bilious headache; her appetite was precarious, and small; indeed, the wonder used to be where, in that tiny body, space could be found for food! Within a twelvemonth, this self-immolated victim to vanity and pain became a mother, rapid symptoms of inflammation of the liver appeared, and in three days she was a corpse, her puny infant being buried with her. The unnatural pressure she had used had prevented that due action of the liver which is indispensable to the health and well-being of the human frame'.

The correct way to fasten a corset to avoid such discomforts is not to lace it too tightly. From the 1870s, you can also wear a loose-fitting uncorseted tea-gown when you're not out and about. Alternatively, visit after the 1880s when the Rational Dress movement starts to campaign against tight corsetry and numerous layers of clothing, and it becomes more acceptable not to wear stays.

Nevertheless, there was still plenty of resistance to more modern types of fashion. In 1899, Lady Harberton brought a court case against the landlady of a Surrey hotel, after she was refused entry to the public coffee room because she was wearing her cycling outfit of Rationals (knickerbockers). The landlady 'thought it was best in the interests of the good order in her house that ladies wearing rational costumes should not be admitted into the public room, which usually at lunch time, would be crowded with men of all sorts, some of whom would make jokes at the expense of the lady as to the size of her ankle'. The case was thrown out but afterwards, Lady Harberton commented: 'I admit that it is probably certain that women will never ordinarily wear knickerbockers. But mark this – short skirts for walking-wear will be a boon that ought to be easily attained, and once attained, cherished like Magna Carta in the British Constitution'.

At first, drawers were crotchless, so the backs and fronts of the legs were not joined together. Although this sounds quite unseemly for Victorian times, it was very practical when visiting the lavatory or using a chamber pot because there was no need to remove any layers of clothing. From the 1880s, 'closed' drawers with seamed legs and a side opening start to be introduced. Alternatively, coloured flannel knickerbockers, often in bright scarlet, can be worn instead of drawers. Women take to Dr Jaeger's pure wool 'combinations' just as positively as men, as they provide some much needed warmth in cold houses and an alternative to a separate chemise and pair of drawers.

Surely no other item of clothing can have been as mercilessly lampooned in the popular press as the crinoline. This is a 'cage' worn underneath one or two petticoats to support a full skirt. Although it's hugely impractical on public transport and crowded streets, the crinoline is actually very comfortable to wear and walk in, especially in hot weather, as the petticoats are kept away from the legs. It is in fashion from the early 1850s to the late 1860s. This style of cage petticoat is also a boon to thieves. According to *The Penny Illustrated Paper* (1862), a servant girl at Chelmarsh, Salop, was suspected of robbing her master. After examining her crinoline, 'it was found that under it she had a belt to which was attached a bonnet, a pair of stays, three skirts, four pair of stockings, two pair of boots, a quantity of muslin, four handkerchiefs, four collars and a gold brooch, all the property of her master and mistress and the boarders in her establishment'.

From about 1868, the bustle replaces the crinoline. Made of steel half-hoops or with a padded pillow arrangement, it projects the shape backwards like a shelf. When wearing a bustle, you will have to lower yourself carefully into a chair, and perch on it instead of sitting back. The straight, sheath-like dresses of this period also make it difficult to walk up and down stairs, or to bend over to pick something up from the floor.

Blouses worn with skirts are introduced in the 1860s for informal wear, and by the 1880s and 1890s, they become very popular. Most skirts have pockets but you can also make use of the detachable pocket, which is tied around the waist under the crinoline or bustle. This is extremely useful for concealing valuables.

Whenever you visit Victorian England, you will reveal considerably more flesh in a fashionably low-cut evening dress than in day wear. In 1837, after his elderly mistress had given a party, footman William Tayler wrote in his diary: 'It's quite disgusting to a modist [sic] eye to see the way the young ladies dress to atract [sic] the notice of the gentlemen. They are nearly naked to the waist, only just a little bit of dress hanging on the shoulder, the breasts are quite exposed except a little bit comeing [sic] up to hide the nipples. Plenty of false haire [sic] and teeth and paint'.

Mrs Florence Ingillson, a Leeds housewife, shared her memories of the attire she wore for the theatre or a ball in the late 1890s in *Leslie Baily's BBC Scrapbook*:

'When I was dressed in my finery I wore three petticoats, the under one of white flannel beautifully embroidered, then a moiré one, and the third of silk with five or six rows of frills – and didn't they take some ironing! The frills had to be goffered with a special iron, like a pair of curling tongs, but when you walked they sounded lovely, they went frou-frou. Underclothes were of silk or wool or cotton. Most girls wore black cotton stockings at sixpence or a shilling a pair; real silk were anything from 10s 6d to £5.

A cloak or mantle will protect you from the elements, while a shawl is an excellent cover-up in milder weather and gloves encase the hands. You can't go out without a hat; up to the 1860s, women wear simple bonnets with pretty trimmings. Small hats, straw versions and bonnets are popular after this time, then in the 1890s, larger hats adorned with feathers and flowers come into fashion. Alterations and new trimmings from the haberdashers can transform a tired, old hat into a brand new one. Women and young girls are adept at doing this for themselves at home.

Walking through muddy streets can quickly take its toll on your skirts and shoes. American visitor David W. Bartlett describes how women keep their clothing clean: 'You will see scores of fine ladies…each suspending her garments gracefully with one hand, just above the reach of the mud, and tripping along on tiptoe with admirable skill, or perhaps walking with wooden clogs under her shoes. Some of them will walk miles in this manner, preserving their dresses and skirts in their original purity'.

This method of walking will take you some time to perfect. Some women also wear pattens or rubber galoshes to protect their shoes from the mud, especially in rural areas. Inevitably, dresses still get muddy and in *Period Piece*, Gwen Raverat recalls the daily bind of keeping walking skirts clean:

> *'It was difficult to walk freely in the heavy tweed "walking skirts" which kept on catching between the knees. Round the bottom of these skirts I had, with my own hands, sewn two and a half yards of "brush braid", to collect the worst of the mud; for they inevitably swept up the roads, however carefully I might hold them up behind…Afterwards the crusted mud had to be brushed off which might take an hour or more to do. There can be no more futile job, imposed by an idiotic convention than that of perpetual skirt-brushing.'*

In the last quarter of the nineteenth century, there is an explosion of interest in physical activities, including playing sports like tennis, croquet and archery, as well as cycling. Clothing, particularly women's, is adapted to give greater freedom of movement. A writer in *Cassell's Family Magazine* (1885) gives the following advice on women's dress for exercise, particularly tricycling:

> *'Shoes, not boots, are de rigueur because shoes give the ankle-tendons and foot-joints free play. To those who have the courage, I would say, abjure petticoats while thus riding, and in their place adopt loose trousers,*

made of a piece of dress, coming well over the knee…all under-clothing should be made of flannel where there is much tricycling – good flannel, all wool, well shrunk. Combination garments are best…The dress should also be in wool [and] particularly trim and neat…Stays can be worn, but anything approaching tight-lacing must be avoided, or a health-giving amusement will be converted into a dangerous one.'

OUTLANDISH FASHIONS

The heavily elaborate clothing worn by the wealthy can be eye-popping in the extreme. The Frenchman Hippolyte Taine believed women's dress, when 'loud and overcharged with ornament, is that of a woman of easy virtue'. According to him, on Sundays in Hyde Park, ladies and girls of the rich middle-classes wear 'hats which look like sprays of rhododendron piled up in a heap, or snow white, or fantastically small, trimmed with clumps of red flowers and enormous ribbons; dresses of purple silk, so very shiny that they reflect the light dazzlingly, or of stiff tulle on a substructure of skirts bristling with embroidery; immense shawls of black lace falling to the heels; immaculate white, or bright purple gloves; gold chains, gold belts with gold clasps; hair lying in a gleaming mass on the nape of the neck. The glare and glitter is brutal: they look as if they have stepped out of a wardrobe and are parading to display the wares of a fancy-goods shop'.

Taine is also critical of the 'swell' or second-rate dandy, describing him as 'a complete fashion plate;

the very latest thing in the most correct taste as regards clothes. Whiskers, moustache and hair just barbered; the man…looks like a hair-dresser's dummy. Motionless attitude, restrained gestures – he must not disturb so much as a fold of his cravat. He wears his clothes as if for show'.

THE WORKING-CLASS WARDROBE

Although they may wear second, third or even fourth-hand clothing, the working classes who need extra money, perhaps to cover a period of sickness or unemployment, can always raise the cash by taking their best garments to the pawnbroker. This is often done week in, week out, with customers queuing up on Saturday night to redeem their parcels ready for Sunday, and returning them again on Monday morning.

Working-class people wear fewer items of clothing than the upper and middle classes, but working men do wear a number of different layers according to C. Willett and Phyllis Cunnington in *The History of Underclothes*. They consist of a white flannel sleeveless vest; a flannel body-belt 'about half a yard wide and stitched across from end to end and tied round with tapes'; and a flannel shirt of 'about three yards of material with sleeves down to the elbows'. This is followed by 'a top shirt made of fine striped flannel or flannelette, and in winter a waistcoat lined with red flannel'. Men wear coloured shirts and drawers on working days, and white on Sundays. They also use loose trouser 'linings', of flannel or twilled calico, made with a wide waistband, and tied round the ankles with tapes, as well as garters of knitted material wound round the top of the stockings, reaching almost to the knee.

CLOTHES-SHOPPING

When Victorian diarists write that they 'bought a gown', it does not usually mean that they purchased a ready-made garment. It is possible to buy part-made dresses but it's still more common to choose dress lengths which are then made up by a dressmaker if they can afford it, or by themselves if not. A contributor to Pat Barr's *I Remember* recalled her mother making clothing for her in the late nineteenth century:

> 'She always bought grey or brown linsey for our dresses and unbleached calico for underclothing and sheets, which she bought at Sewell's drapers shops which stood at the corner of Bishops Stortford Road, Great Dunmow. They would allow her a penny in the shilling discount. At this shop the main entrance was for the quality and a side entrance up some steps for the poorer class.
>
> 'As soon as my sister and I could sew we had to hem the bottoms of our chemises and holland pinafores. My mother made our dresses and Father's shirts which had eight gussets, two at the neck, two at the wrist and two at the side and underarm. The back of the shirt would be gathered into the neck to give freedom of movement for the swing of scythe or billhook. Mother would buy my sister and me little straw hats with a wreath of artificial flowers on them which, in winter, were exchanged for ribbons.'

The invention of the sewing-machine naturally led to the development of ready-to-wear garments in the 1860s. However, when tight corseting is in fashion, it is extremely difficult to get the sizing right for women. Jay's of London (which specialised in mourning wear) was advertising 'completely ready-made dresses in 1866', according to Alison Adburgham in *Shops and Shopping*. Jay's claimed that their 'self-expanding bodice' overcame the 'deviations from the female norm without having to stock dresses in many different measurements'.

Ready-to-wear clothes can be mass-produced, making them cheaper than tailored garments. They become extremely popular with the middle and working classes, especially when persuaded by advertisements like this one for Gosling's Clothing Warehouse in Ulverston, dating from 1882. It boasts

'A splendid Fit, beautifully and firmly made, and the Prices cheaper than "City" firms charge you'. Ready-made suits in the newest styles for boys are available from 3/11; for youths from 13/6 and men from 21/6.' There is also an order department for made-to-measure garments. All you had to do was leave your measurements and choose from 'a choice assortment of all the newest designs in Tweed Suitings, Worsted Suitings & c'.

Then, as now, young women and girls like to look fashionable and they eagerly pore over the latest fashion plates in magazines and periodicals. Yet, with so many layers and pieces of clothing required for an outfit, looking good doesn't come cheap. Luckily, the same magazines, offering a window into the world of fashion straight from Paris, also provide helpful tips on how to be stylish when watching the pennies. In an article called 'Some Hints on Economy in Dress', *Cassell's Family Magazine* (1885) provides advice for ladies on how to dress well without spending too much money:

> *'A very good rule for those...who are obliged to study economy is to confine themselves to one or two colours as, for instance, black or blue, or brown, and white, so that one set of ribbons, waistbands, &c., and one hat or bonnet, may be worn with two or more dresses.'*

Although winter coats, cloaks and mantles are expensive articles, 'it is true economy to buy them very good, but not of any striking pattern or colour. A plaid coat or Newmarket will soon look remarkable, but one of plain cloth may be worn year after year, and look well to the last.' The old adage that you get what you pay for rang true in Victorian times. 'An Old Stager' advised visitors to London to 'have nothing to do with cheap clothes, which are always dear in the end...there is great danger from contagion from the unwholesome places in which most of the cheap clothes are made up'.

For women in rural areas, who did not have access to haberdashers and were not in touch with the latest fashions, the arrival of the packman was an exciting event. This itinerant vendor was essentially a pedlar carrying dress lengths, shawls, collars, handkerchiefs and other accessories. In towns, he sold to fashion-conscious servants who could not afford shop prices.

The packman who visited Flora Thompson's home

village of Juniper Hill in the 1880s is remembered in *Lark Rise to Candleford*:

'He would turn aside from the turnpike and come plodding down the narrow hamlet road, an old white-headed, white-bearded man, still hale and rosy, although almost bent double under the heavy, black canvas-covered pack he carried strapped on his shoulders. "Anything out of the pack today?" he would ask at each house, and, at the least encouragement, fling down his load and open it on the doorstep.

'He carried a tempting variety of goods: dress-lengths and shirt-lengths and remnants to make up for the children; aprons and pinafores, plain and fancy; corduroys for the men, and coloured scarves and ribbons for Sunday wear. Few of the hamlet women could afford to test the quality of his piece goods; cottons or tapes, or a paper of pins, were their usual purchases, but his dress lengths and other fabrics were of excellent quality.'

As a visitor from modern times, you may find it easier and less cumbersome to visit during the 1890s when women can wear uncorseted tea-gowns and men can opt for less formal sporting jackets without looking out of place.

Now that you're correctly attired, you should be able to pass unnoticed on a busy street, but don't forget your hat!

Chapter Four
Food and Drink

*'Next to this stood baked potatoes, brown and crisp;
and after this, peas-pudding, in warm and heavy lumps
upon a cabbage-leaf. My regular shop used to cook
twice a day; once at twelve in the morning, and again
at eight in the evening. No delicacy that I could have
had at home was half so choice in my eyes as these
penny-worths of pudding and potatoes, bought amidst
a crowd of cabmen, carters, and coalheavers, and dirty
women receiving their dinners and suppers in yellow
basins – meat, pudding, greens, potatoes, gravey [sic],
and mustard, all mixed together.'*
(John Hollingshead, *Ways of Life*, 1861)

When visiting a foreign country, most people will
venture to try some of the local cuisine. However, in
Victorian England, you'll have a battle on your hands
to avoid suspect food and contaminated drinks. This
is especially true in the hot summer months when flies
swarm and leave deposits on uncovered provisions. If
you're a vegetarian, then you'll really struggle, if not
starve! Meat, and the smell of it, is everywhere, although
vegetarian restaurants do become a fashionable fad in
English cities from the 1880s onwards.

On your visit, you'll quickly discover that fast food
is nothing new. There's a proliferation of street vendors

selling a wide variety of food and drink, so it's unlikely that you will ever go hungry. Part of the reason for the large numbers of vendors is the fact that those from the poorest classes have no cooking facilities at home or anywhere to store food, and therefore their only means of getting a hot meal is to buy it ready-made. Of course, this does mean eating in the streets, often in cold weather.

Henry Mayhew highlights the fact that both men and women, and especially boys, buy their meals day after day from street vendors in *London Labour and the London Poor* (1861): 'The coffee stall supplies a warm breakfast; shell-fish of all kinds tempt to a luncheon; hot-eels or pea-soup, flanked by a potato "all hot", serve for a dinner; and cakes and tarts, or nuts and oranges, with many varieties of pastry, confectionary [sic] and fruit, woo to indulgence in a dessert; while for supper there is a sandwich, a meat pudding or a "trotter"'. Other favourite foods of the working classes include pickled whelks, oysters and fried fish; ham sandwiches, hot green peas and kidney puddings; and beef, mutton, kidney, and eel pies. Oysters were plentiful in Victorian times, so much so that they are part of the staple diet for the poor. Sam Weller in *The Pickwick Papers* declares, 'Poverty and oysters always seem to go together'.

Costermongers sell fruit and vegetables from a barrow, and visit the streets in their 'patch' in the course of the day. In *Ways of Life* (1861), John Hollingshead recalls that although there were hundreds of fruit stalls, he only ever bought from one which was run by an old lady:

'She sold ribstone pippins, two for a penny; hard Brazil nuts, that punished your teeth fearfully to crack them, and, sometimes, would not give in, except under the heel of the boot; she sold, occasionally, curds and whey ladled out into a saucer with a clean, broad shell; and she sold slices of sweet cocoa-nut. In the winter-time, she had a chimney-pot pan, with holes in it, full of burning charcoal, at which she warmed her hands and roasted chesnuts [sic].'

Both savoury and sweet pies are hugely popular, and you can buy them from a pie shop or an itinerant pieman. Women, however, seldom buy pies in the streets. Henry Mayhew describes street pastry as having a 'strong flavour' which he attributes to 'the use of rancid or old butter...or to the substitution of lard, dripping or some congenial substance'.

When you're out and about exploring the streets, why not try to 'toss the pieman'? This is a favourite game of costermongers' boys. If the street pieman wins the toss, he receives a penny without giving a pie; if he loses, he hands it over for nothing. The pieman never tosses, but always calls heads or tails to the customer. One pieman that Henry Mayhew interviewed claimed, 'Very few people buy without tossing, and the boys in particular. Gentlemen 'out on the spree' at the late public-houses will frequently toss when they don't want the pies, and when they win they will amuse themselves by throwing the pies at one another, or at me'.

In the summer, there are ice cream vendors with their gaily painted barrows; most of them claim to be Italian. They bang their cart lids and shout, "Hokey Pokey, penny a lump!" to get your attention. But beware the ice cream… It's made in the most insanitary conditions, is full of bacteria and is often the cause of outbreaks of food poisoning. When ice cream is examined by scientists in 1895, it is found to contain a cocktail of nasty ingredients including 'bed bugs, bugs' legs, fleas, straw, human hair, cats' and dogs' hairs, coal dust, woollen and linen fibres, [and] tobacco'. If you want to try Victorian ice cream, then the safer option is to eat it in a restaurant or tea-room.

Henry Mayhew also observes the huge range of drinks offered by street sellers. There is 'tea, coffee, and cocoa; ginger-beer, lemonade, Persian sherbet…; hot elder cordial or wine; peppermint water; curds and whey; water; rice milk and milk in the parks'. Persian sherbet is the trade-name for a type of fizzy drink, which resembles lemonade, and is made with water, bicarbonate of soda, cream of tartar, sugar and flavouring. In England's temperate climate, coffee stalls are very popular. The stall-holder has three or four large tin cans, containing hot milk, tea, coffee and sometimes cocoa. Beneath each can is a small iron fire-pot, under which charcoal is kept burning. Some coffee stalls are covered over with tarpaulin, like a tent, to protect customers from the elements; all are brightly lit after dark to attract customers.

According to Mayhew, these vendors sometimes start work at midnight to cater for the 'nightwalkers', the 'fast gentlemen and loose girls', while those who begin at three or four in the morning target working men looking for breakfast. Coffee stalls also sell food such as bread and butter, cake, and ham sandwiches.

The drinks are served in mugs, or cups and saucers, and customers drink next to the stall: there are no disposable cups! Coffee, tea or cocoa are 1d per mug or ½d for half a mug. Chicory is mixed with coffee to make it go further.

Milk is brought round the streets either by a pony carrying churns in a cart, or a donkey with a can in each pannier. In both cases there is a dipper to measure out the required amounts and customers bring their own receptacles to be filled. Richard Jefferies describes the milk leaving Wiltshire by train in *Hodge and His Masters* (1880): 'Each tin bears a brazen badge engraved with the name of the milkman who will retail its contents in distant London. It may be delivered to the countess in Belgravia, and reach her dainty lip in the morning chocolate, or it may be eagerly swallowed up by the half-starved children of some back court in the purlieus of Seven Dials'. The main line of the Great Western Railway running through Berkshire and Wiltshire was nicknamed the 'Milky Way', with 20 million gallons of milk each year brought into the capital by 1880. The easier transportation of milk means that cows and dairies vanish from London.

ALCOHOL AND ALCOHOLISM

You can buy alcoholic drinks from a wide range of places in Victorian England, including gin palaces or public houses, beer-houses and licensed shops like grocers or confectioners. It's easy to see why drunkenness is such a problem in the poorer districts as there are several beer-houses on every street, making it very difficult to avoid temptation! Temperance workers estimated that in the middle of the nineteenth century 'more was spent every year on drink than on rent – an average of £3 per person', according to Christopher Hibbert.

Official figures of the 1870s indicate that there were about ten pints of spirits, four pints of wine and 275 pints of beer drunk each year for every man, woman and child. In many trades, it is common to pay workers' wages in a public house 'in whose profits the employers had an interest'. This clearly exacerbates the complex relationship the working classes have with alcohol, and new laws are introduced to prohibit this practice.

On visiting England in 1847, John Henry Sherburne, an American, looked into one of the gin palaces which he claimed were on every square in London 'brilliantly illuminated at night with costly gas-burners'. He comments that they were mostly frequented by miserable women and children, 'single and married, of all ages, surrounding the beautiful marble counter, with each a small pitcher or bottle in one hand, waiting their turn, the other holding out a few pence, with looks of greedy anxiety...Gin was their bread, meat, their all'.

Sherburne does not seem to have taken into account that many of these women, and certainly the children, fetch gin for their fathers and husbands. He claims the 'palaces' were countenanced and protected by the London authorities because the Corporation received an income from their licences.

You can get as drunk as you like behind closed doors, but if you're found intoxicated in public, this could land you in serious trouble. Short prison sentences with hard labour are meted out to persistent drunk and disorderly offenders. By the end of the nineteenth century, habitual drunks who commit criminal offences while under the influence are forcibly detained in reformatories for inebriates.

The Frenchman Hippolyte Taine comments on the English taste for alcohol in *Notes on England* (1872):

> *'with the wines they drink, port and sherry very full and strong and, furthermore, blended with brandy – a practice which ruins their subtler qualities. But if they were pure the English would find them insipid: our wines of Bordeaux, and even of Burgundy, are too light for them. In the middle-classes ale, stout and porter are preferred, and above all "brandy-and-water", a kind of grog which is one half spirits. In order to please them a drink must be harsh and burning; their palates need to be scratched or scraped'.*

EATING OUT

From rough-and-ready chop houses and public houses, elegant tea-rooms and refreshment rooms, through to comprehensive oyster bars and high-class restaurants, there's a wide range of places to eat during your visit. The widest choice can be found in the cities. In Birmingham, *Kirk's Popular Guide* (1889) recommends Pope's (called 'the Vatican' by the proprietor) as the great oyster bar of Birmingham: 'Here you can get a snack of fish of all kinds in season, and of the best quality. Pope's is the supper room for after theatre parties, and is largely patronised as such'. Pope's is at 3 Cannon Street close to New Street and it offers 'real Whitstable natives, best Dutch natives, and other Oysters'. Chops and steaks are also served, and high quality ales, wines and cigars are available.

Pope's restaurant offers table d'hôte between 5pm and 8.30pm for 3s 6d. The menu includes olives stuffed with anchovies; soups (macaroni or hare); fish (boiled turbot and lobster sauce or fried eels); entrées (mutton cutlets and tomato sauce or sauti of rabbit); joints (roast gosling); game (partridge or wild duck); sweets (sweet omelette); savoury (devilled sardines on toast); and cheese and salad. If you want to try this out, you'd better have indigestion pills at the ready.

The guide also recommends a different type of eatery: Pattison's, the 'great resort for afternoon tea'. Advertisements stress that 'London people send down for Pattison's pastry when they give parties'. There are three establishments in Birmingham and 'their place of business at the lower end of New Street is crowded in the morning with ladies purchasing supplies of pastry, and in the evening with ladies and gentlemen taking afternoon tea'. The tea is 'the best that can be brewed' and the attendants are 'young ladies noted for good looks and courtesy'.

Chop houses are particularly popular with men, but one establishment advertising in *Cornish's Stranger's Guide through Birmingham* (1858) is keen to appeal to women: 'One visit to Allday's Celebrated Chop House and Corn Exchange Dining Rooms No. 30 Union Street, a few doors from High Street and Union Passage Will Prove that the prominent considerations rigidly adhered to at this Establishment are First-rate quality of Meat, Economy of Charge, Strict attention to Cleanliness, and also to the Wishes and Comforts of the Guests'. There are separate refreshment rooms for ladies, and hot joints are ready from 12 until 4pm. Another Birmingham chop house is the Waterloo Bar, 'a splendidly fitted and decorated luncheon bar, famous for its chops and steaks, and the resort of business men'. There are four billiard tables, indicating that the Waterloo Bar's target clientele is decidedly male.

If you want to save a bit of money on dining out, take a tip from Nathaniel Hawthorne. In his *English Note-Books*, he recalls visiting Coventry for the day in 1855: 'We went to the Red Lion, and had a luncheon of cold lamb and cold pigeon pie. This is the best way of dining at English hotels – to call the meal a luncheon, in which case you will get as good or better a variety than if it were a dinner, and at less than half the cost'.

Follow your nose and you will easily find inexpensive snacks down the side alleys of towns and cities. George Frederick Pardon offers useful advice in *The Popular Guide to London and its Suburbs*. If you want very cheap food 'and not particularly nice, you may find it in almost every bye-street, where hot joints smoke and steam in the windows, and you may get your appetite appeased by the scent of the dishes before you have put a morsel in your mouth. Remember Mr Punch's advice to diners – What to eat, drink and avoid: Turtle, Champagne and Ham Sandwiches for a penny!'

Refreshment rooms are a particular feature of city streets, railway stations, department stores and tourist attractions like museums and exhibitions. 'You go to a refreshment-room, help yourself, state what you have taken, and pay. Just the same is done in the City restaurants at lunch-time', writes Max O'Rell in *John Bull and his Island*. 'Gentlemen generally eat standing up: they are served on the instant; there is no time to lose; no serviettes – you wipe your mouth with your handkerchief. Lunch is despatched in ten minutes. You might almost hear a pin drop while this roomful of merchants, clerks, etc. are taking their mid-day repast'.

At the 1851 Great Exhibition, there are three separate refreshment rooms for different budgets and social classes, where light and moderate refreshments are served. No hot meals are available, nor are intoxicating drinks. 'Visitors consumed more than a million bottles of soft drinks (Messrs Schweppes had the contract) and 1,804,718 buns – half of them Bath buns,' according to Elizabeth Burton in *The Early Victorians at Home*. She adds that jelly had previously been 'the prerogative of those with money who kept a good table. Now, for the first time, jelly appeared in public and within the reach of everyone with a few pence to spend'.

When Nathaniel Hawthorne and his family visited the Crystal Palace in September 1855:

'The first thing we did, before fairly getting into the palace, was to sit down in a large ante-hall, and get some bread and butter and a pint of Bass's pale ale, together with a cup of coffee for S__. This was the best refreshment we could find at that spot; but farther within we found abundance of refreshment-rooms, and John Bull and his wife and family at fifty little round tables, busily engaged with cold fowl, cold beef, ham, tongue, and bottles of ale and stout, and half-pint decanters of sherry.'

Dearman Birchall, a squire and landowner, was not impressed with the refreshment rooms at the Crystal Palace when he visited in May 1872. He wrote in his diary: 'We refreshed ourselves at the 2/8 cold colation room; never will I visit there again – 15/- for two tankards of horrid claret cup, 10/- for ditto cider and nothing nice to eat'.

Even if you dine out at a high-class restaurant, don't expect particularly good quality food. Hippolyte Taine observes that:

> 'excepting in the very best clubs and among continentalised English people, who have a French or Italian chef, [the cooking] is devoid of savour. I have dined, deliberately, in twenty different inns, from the highest to the lowest, in London and elsewhere: huge helpings of greasy meat and vegetable without sauce; one is amply and wholesomely fed, but one can take no pleasure in eating. The best restaurant in Liverpool cannot dress a chicken. If your palate demands enjoyment, here is a dish of pimentos, peppers, condiments, Indian vinegars: on one occasion I carelessly put two drops into my mouth. I might just as well have been swallowing a red-hot coal. At Greenwich, having had a helping of ordinary "whitebait", I helped myself to more but from another dish: it was a dish of curried whitebait – excellent for taking the skin off one's tongue'.

When eating out, you'll quickly realise that women are a rare sight in restaurants. *The American Stranger's Guide to London and Liverpool at Table* (1859) highlights the fact that in London and other cities, it is difficult to find restaurants where women can dine. 'It is true that some have been opened where gentlemen may take their wives and daughters, but it has not yet become a recognised custom, although at Blackwall, Greenwich, Hampton Court, Windsor, Slough, [and] Richmond, ladies are to be found as in the Parisian Cafes, and in London at "Verey's" in Pall Mall and Regent Street; but to give a private dinner with ladies, it is necessary to go to the "Albion" or "London Tavern" where nothing can exceed the magnificence of the rooms'.

If you're travelling by railway on an excursion, take your own provisions if you can. Although there are refreshment rooms at stations along the main routes, these places are always crowded and even if you can get a seat, you'll be watching the clock to make sure you don't miss your connection. Later in the nineteenth century, long distance trains start to offer refreshment baskets.

Molly Hughes recalled her family's long railway journeys from London to Cornwall in her memoir *A London Child of the 1870s:* 'Didcot had one definite pleasure. We knew that little boys would be going up and down the platform singing out, "Banbury cakes! Banbury cakes!" And Mother would crane out and buy some'. After Didcot came Swindon: 'Considering our early breakfast, or lack of it, the refreshment-room at Swindon was a land of Canaan, and the hot soup all round is still a joyful memory'.

The family's lunch was in a bulging basket on the luggage rack:

'for food as a species of rapture nothing compares with sandwiches, eggs, pasties, and turnovers, doled out one

by one from napkins, when the supply is severely limited. Oranges in summer were unknown then, as well as all the foreign apples and other fruit to be had in London today. We had to slake our thirst with acid-drops and a tiny ration of lemonade. If by chance a fellow passenger remained we always managed to do some little barter of biscuits or sweets, because strange food is even more pleasant than one's own.'

DINNER PARTIES

The upper and middle classes enjoy giving dinner parties at home, which are aimed at impressing their friends and business contacts, and cementing their place in society. If you're invited to a dinner party, don't be surprised to see a large number of courses and a sparkling array of silverware – remember that the occasion is primarily designed as a display of wealth. The aspirational *Book of Household Management* (1861) by Mrs Isabella Beeton is hugely influential on the way in which the middle classes dine and entertain. She suggests set menus for dinner parties with varying numbers of guests and at different times of the year, and even offers ideas for plain family dinners.

Dinner *à la Russe* becomes popular during the 1860s; these are distinct from ordinary dinners in which each course is served by a butler or footman. Instead, the dishes are cut up on the sideboard and handed round to the guests. As a large number of servants is needed to carve joints and attend to the guests, dinner *à la Russe* is not suitable for smaller homes. Mrs Beeton stresses that the table should be 'laid with flowers and plants in fancy flowerpots down the middle, together with some of the dessert dishes'.

AVOIDING CONTAMINATED FOOD

Adulterated food can catch out unwitting Victorian customers and make them seriously ill, so you will be especially at risk. The problem is that nothing is as it seems. For instance, ground bones, plaster, lime and pipe-clay are often added to bread, as is alum. The latter increases its weight and adds whiteness, but it can cause severe indigestion.

It would be wise to follow the advice of *The Magazine of Domestic Economy* (1842) which urges its readers to deal 'only with full-price reputable shops' because 'the difference of a farthing a pound (which is all that exists …between the good and the to-be-suspected article) is hardly worth the saving'. The publication does acknowledge that those 'who live from hand to mouth, and deal (perhaps, on credit) at chandlers' shops have no choice but to choose the cheapest bread'. This is yet another instance of the advantages the wealthier social classes have in retaining good health.

Adulteration, though, is not confined to bread. Confectionery is bright and attractive because potentially lethal salts of copper and lead are used to colour sweets. Beer, that staple of the poorer classes, is diluted and then adulterated with vitriol and cocolus indicus which can cause convulsions, gastroenteritis and over-stimulate the respiratory system.

You will usually find milk in the countryside to be

more pure than that sold in urban areas. Although it is routinely watered down, the squalid conditions in which cows live in towns and cities has more to do with its lack of quality than any adulteration. According to *The Magazine of Domestic Economy*, 'the state of unnatural confinement and restraint in which cows are generally kept up the back yards and close alleys...is sufficient to account for much of the badness of milk – its poverty and yet its strong tendency to putrefaction'. Mrs Layton recalls her childhood in Bethnal Green in the 1860s in Margaret Llewelyn Davies' *Life As We Have Known It:* 'At the back of the house a cowkeeper and dairyman kept in large sheds about forty milk cows...The cows were turned out every day into a large yard which was only divided from our premises by a low wall. The smell was at times intolerable, and the flies in the summer were a perfect plague'.

Many shopkeepers claim to be unaware of the potentially fatal consequences of adulterating the food they sell. A case of poisonous Bath buns was reported in 1859 at Clifton, Gloucestershire. Six pupils at a boarding school bought the cakes from a confectioner's shop but 'in the evening all six were seized with violent sickness, and presented the symptoms of having partaken of some poisonous substance'. The local surgeon was called in to prescribe the necessary remedies but two of them continued so ill that they were not expected to survive. Fortunately, 'after great suffering', they all recovered. After some of the unconsumed buns were analysed, 'it was found that each of them contained seven grains of chromate of lead, which was used as a cheap substitute for eggs, for the purpose of colouring the buns'. The confectioner admitted having used this preparation for some time, without being aware of its injurious effects, and it was supposed that in this instance, a larger dose than usual was, through carelessness, placed in the buns.

Until 1875, there was very little control over the food and drink sold to the public. Under the Sale of Food and Drugs Act, passed in that year, inspectors had the power to sample food and drugs, and to test them for adulteration. This was the beginning of trading standards legislation to protect customers. If you visit in the 1880s or 1890s, there is a reduced risk of being sold adulterated food or drink, and even if you do succumb to food poisoning, medical advances mean it can usually be treated successfully.

Now that you know where to find the best food and how to avoid the worst, it's time to get to grips with Victorian public transport.

Chapter Five
Getting Around

'Costermongers and itinerant vendors all along the pavement; the houses covered with signboards and inscriptions; busy crowds on either side; omnibuses rushing to and fro in the centre of the road, and all around that indescribable bewildering noise of human voices, carriage-wheels and horses' hooves, which pervades the leading streets into crowded cities.'
(Max Schlesinger, *Saunterings In and About London*, 1853)

It's rush hour: the clip-clop of horses' hooves and the thunderous sound of carriage and cab wheels over cobbles seem deafening to your ears. In the distance, there is a sharp whistle and a chuff-chuff of steam as a train leaves the station a few streets away. Everyone is in a hurry and they all know where they're going, but the transport seems entirely alien to you. That's because, apart from the steam train, it's all horse-drawn until the late 1890s.

If you visit towards the end of Queen Victoria's reign, you'll have more options for getting around than when she first came to the throne. In 1837, the stagecoach was king for long-distance journeys and 'railway mania' was still in its infancy.

TAKING THE STAGECOACH

To experience the open road, you should take a stagecoach journey. Coaching inns (or stages) are the hub of stagecoach activity, providing extensive stables, fresh horses and refreshments for passengers en route. They are also the principal hotels for the towns in which they are located. On a major route, there can be as many as 15 or 20 coaches passing through every day, from early in the morning to late at night. Driven by one coachman, each coach is usually pulled by four horses (known as a four-in-hand). Horses are changed every ten to 15 miles.

If you want to travel by stagecoach, it's important to reserve a place in advance at a booking office. First-class passengers sit inside, while cheaper tickets are available for those who perch on the roof and are exposed to the elements. The most coveted place is the box-seat next to the coachman. John Hollingshead recalled in *Odd Journeys In and Out of London* (1860) how this seat was only obtained after 'many weeks' booking and many shillings' fee'. The passenger 'who got it by dint of patience, forethought and capital, was an object of envy to his fellow-voyagers the journey through. He was a comfortable man, because (in the winter-time) in addition to his own shawls and rugs, he had the extra protection of the coachman's leather apron. He was a happy man...because he was occasionally entrusted with the ribbons or reins during certain rests'.

When your coach draws up at an inn, if you're not an inside passenger, the guard will help you down from the roof of the vehicle using a ladder. You'll notice a flurry of activity from the inn itself with porters rushing to and fro with luggage, and ostlers looking after the horses and harnesses, and getting fresh ones ready. Inside, the staff will be ready and waiting to receive you and the other passengers. If you're not staying the night, you can use the coffee-room reserved especially for you.

To travel 'post' means to go by the mail coach, usually at night. This is a much faster but more expensive journey, since its main purpose is to deliver the mail, and the comfort of passengers is secondary to this. There are few stops, except to change horses. Victorian diarists frequently record entries such as 'posted across country' or 'took the post'.

John Henry Sherburne, an American, visited England in 1847:

> 'From Gloucester to Bristol is thirty-six miles; and wishing to see the country, I took an outside seat on the stage-coach – also for variety [sic] sake – fare four shillings. The road is fine, the coachman always polite and attentive, for his own interest [sic] sake, receiving from each passenger one shilling, which is all the pay he receives, as no wages are allowed stage-coach drivers in England, by the proprietors, while the guard is well paid for winding his bugle on approaching a stopping-place.'

The coachmen were 'noted for the care and kind attention to their horses, at all times and seasons'.

If the stagecoach you're travelling in or on is overloaded, then you may have to get out and walk with the other passengers up steep hills to spare the horses. Overloading could also lead to accidents such as overturning. When he travelled from Grasmere to Windermere by stagecoach in 1855, Nathaniel Hawthorne commented:

> 'The coach was greatly overburdened with outside passengers – fifteen in all, beside the four insiders – and one of the fifteen formed the apex of an immense pile of luggage on top. It seems to me miraculous that we did not topple over, the road being so hilly and uneven, and the driver, I suspect, none the steadier for his visits to all the tap-rooms along the route from Cockermouth. There was a tremendous vibration of the coach now and then; and I saw that, in case of our going over, I should be flung headlong against the high stone fence that bordered most of the road...As far as apprehension goes, I had rather travel from Maine to Georgia by rail, than from Grasmere to Windermere by stage-coach.'

TRAVELLING BY TRAIN

Steam railways are not a Victorian invention, but it is during this period that the railway network expands across Britain, changing the landscape forever. By 1852, only three important English towns do not have a railway station: Hereford, Yeovil and Weymouth. Yet, opposition to the railways is fierce, especially among those in the coaching industry. In one unnamed small country town in the 1840s, a main railway line was constructed nearby and a branch line was mapped out to the town itself. The development was not welcomed by the locals. John Hollingshead recalled: 'I saw with my own eyes (and dared not interfere) one of the early

71

surveyors seized by indignant villagers connected with the coaching interest, and ducked in a horse-pond'.

Pure ignorance lay behind some of the resistance. In 1831, *Berrow's Worcester Journal* reported that a Northamptonshire farmer had refused assent to the proposed London and Birmingham Railway on his land because 'the columns of smoke thrown out by the Steam-Engines would injure the fleeces of his sheep'. The newspaper argued that this demonstrated 'there are people who need to be told that the Loco-motive Steam-Engines use coke for fuel, and that they emit no smoke'.

In April 1839, Eliza Nutt Harwood, daughter of a farmer and publican, had her first sight of a steam engine moving along the line near her home in Beeston, Nottinghamshire. In her diary, she recorded that it 'moved majestickly [sic] and beautifully along. There was a very great many peopal [sic] to see them pass. It is a very handsom [sic] engine'. Eliza had attended a lecture about locomotive engines and railways with her father the previous year, so the idea was not new to her but she was impressed nonetheless.

Early steam trains could reach speeds of between 15 and 20 miles per hour. As no-one really knew the effect that travelling so quickly would have on the human body, there was plenty of scaremongering about. One medical authority warned: 'All persons travelling on railways are strongly recommended not to fix their eyes too intently on objects which they pass, as doing so is likely to prove both painful and injurious to those most delicate organs. This is especially urged to those who may have a tendency towards a determination of blood to the head'.

Yet the speed and convenience of railways appealed most to travellers. The Liverpool to Manchester railway opened in 1830 and five months later, more than 100,000 passengers had travelled on the line. *Berrow's Worcester Journal* compared the speed of the train with the stagecoach: 'Passengers are conveyed between Liverpool and Manchester in two hours for 4s 6d, instead of in four or five hours by the stage coaches for ten or twelve shillings...The most rapid coaches travel at the rate of nine or ten miles an hour, a speed which in three or four years destroys the horses'. The immediate consequence of the opening of the railway in London was reduced activity at the coach-offices. Newspapers carried daily advertisements announcing the sale of horses, which had previously pulled stagecoaches.

From 1838, you could travel from Birmingham to London by railway, starting at Curzon-Street Station and terminating at Euston Grove. At first, the line was not fully complete and the section between Rugby and Denbigh Hall (near Bletchley) had to be travelled by stagecoach, adding four hours to the journey time. Here, passengers rejoined the train for the remainder of the journey which, in total, took eight and a half hours. The fares were 30 shillings inside, and 20 shillings outside or second-class. There was no third-class option at this point.

It was not until 17 September 1838 that the whole line between London and Birmingham was opened, and the first London train arrived at Curzon Street (the precursor to the later New Street station). The rigmarole of transferring between train and stagecoach and back again was now done away with.

The first public train on this line left London at ten past eight in the morning, arriving in Birmingham at a quarter to one. The duration of the journey was four hours 35 minutes.

Catching a train

On arrival in Victorian England, one of the first things you should buy is *Bradshaw's Monthly Railway Guide*, which is indispensable for planning journeys by train. You can buy it from any newspaper stall at or near a railway station; look for the distinctive yellow wrapper. Published monthly from 1841, it compiles all the timetables and fares from the various railway companies. By 1845, the original eight pages had grown to 32 and in 1898, it was a whopping 946 pages! It also includes hackney coach and cab fares from all the principal railway stations, which should ensure you're not ripped off by a cabman.

When you arrive at a railway station, you will need to decide which carriage you want to travel in. Railways reinforce the Victorian social structure and you will have a choice of first, second and third-class carriages; the latter were not offered until late 1838. Children under the age of ten are charged at half-price, and only infants unable to walk could travel for free. Your choice of carriage may depend on the weather. Compartments are unheated, even in first-class, although there is a foot warmer for these better-off passengers. Elizabeth Burton points out in *The Early Victorians at Home* how noxious these carriages are at night, as they are illuminated 'by an evil-smelling and dripping oil lamp fixed in the roof'. The cushions in first-class carriages are also inclined to catch the dust from the steam engine.

Second-class carriages have a roof but are open at the sides. Wrapping up warm with a rug, cap and cloak is essential, as is an umbrella. You will also need to take your own cushion. 'A Constant Traveller' wrote to the *Leicester Chronicle* in 1843 about the 'miserably cold and wretchedly devised carriages'. He commented: 'The day was windy and wet, the rain poured in so heavily that a pool of water above an inch deep deluged the floor, and...most of the passengers...were wet through, not being provided with any protective clothing'.

You'll find that the early third-class carriages are little more than cattle trucks with no roof and hard wooden seats. This mirrors the experience of third-class passengers on the top of a stagecoach, but railway travellers also have to contend with the hazards of smoke, soot and cinders. A passenger travelling from London to Liverpool via Birmingham on the Grand Junction line wrote to the *Leeds Mercury* in 1841, complaining of the third-class accommodation: 'I witnessed several instances in and near the carriage in which I was placed, of clothing, umbrellas &c being burnt and utterly spoiled by the ashes from the engine, some pieces the size of a walnut being precipitated, red-hot, into the midst of us. In fact, on arriving at Birmingham, if the seat and floor of that part of the carriage in which I rode had been swept, not less than half a pint of cinders might have been gathered'.

Despite the sub-standard accommodation, railway

travel was hugely popular. According to the *Railway Times*, in the first six months of 1839, the London to Birmingham railway carried 267,527 people. In eight months, the line between Sheffield and Rotherham attracted 330,000 passengers. *The Morning Chronicle* (1844) reported: 'Last week, some of the Yorkshire railways offered the public of the West Riding a trip down to Liverpool and back for a few shillings a place, and though the accommodation in the carriages was no better than that given to cattle on the Liverpool and Manchester line, yet no less than five thousand persons availed themselves of this opportunity of visiting Liverpool and the sea!'

With the development of railways, cheap pleasure excursions became common, especially on Sundays. *Household Narrative* reported that on Sunday 15 September 1850, 'three thousand persons went by the Great Western from Paddington to Bath and Bristol. On the preceding Sunday there was an excursion train from Bristol and other places to Windsor – about a thousand persons were conveyed'. There was great opposition from the clergy of Bath and Bristol, who complained about the demoralizing effect of the excursions 'and of scenes of riot and disorderly conduct in the streets by an influx of persons having no regard for the sacredness of the Sabbath, with the temptation held out to townsmen to join in these misdoings'.

After 1844, you'll notice a roof on all third-class carriages which railway companies were forced to provide under new legislation. At least one train every weekday had to run for third-class passengers, stopping at every station along the line. From this time, lighting is also provided in third-class carriages although there is only a single oil lamp per carriage, compared with several in each first-class carriage.

Max O'Rell praises England's swift and excellent trains in *John Bull and his Island* (1884): 'This is the result of competition. You can go from London to Manchester by five different lines. Each company tries to obtain your patronage by offering you more advantages than the others'. The sheer number of different railway companies can be confusing, and if you are unsure about which line to take, consult your *Bradshaw's* or ask a member of staff. The Central Station in New Street, Birmingham was built to accommodate traffic from the London and North Western, the Midland, the Stour Valley and South Staffordshire lines.

Bradshaw's Handbook for Tourists (1863) described the station: 'If the reader notice the turmoil and bustle created by the excitement of the arrival and departure of trains, the trampling of crowds of passengers, the transport of luggage, the ringing of bells, and the noise of two or three hundred porters and workmen, he will retain a recollection of the extraordinary scene witnessed daily at the Birmingham Central Railway Station'.

When you buy your ticket, you will have the option to pay threepence extra for insurance. If there was an accident and you were killed, the railway company would pay your heirs the sum of a thousand pounds in compensation. Also, unless you pay sixpence to book your luggage in, the railway company will take no responsibility for it. If your luggage weighs more than 100 lbs, you will have to pay an excess charge of one pence per pound. The best advice is therefore to travel light, perhaps restricting yourself to one carpet bag with a leather or parchment label – cards are apt to come off.

At first, there were no vans for luggage or the guard, so both travelled on the roof. The 'guard' was in charge of the train, the name being a relic from coaching times. Later, luggage was placed on or in the carriage in which the passenger travelled.

Only first-class passengers had seat numbers issued with their tickets, so you will not be able to reserve a seat as you could in a stagecoach if you are travelling second or third-class. It's best to be early to avoid a scrum for an empty carriage. If you are travelling alone, it is more than likely that someone will strike up a conversation with you in the railway carriage or at the station. To many Victorians, this was an annoying and unsought part of railway travelling. 'An Old Stager' advised: 'It is well to have a newspaper in your hand, to resort to in case tiresome people will talk'. You can buy a paper from one of W. H. Smith's railway bookstalls; the first was opened at Euston in 1848. Don't forget to buy a folding paper-knife at the same time, as newspapers and periodicals are sold uncut until the 1870s.

As you wait on the platform before getting on the train, listen out for the signal bell which is your cue to find a carriage and a seat without delay. You need to take care when choosing a compartment. Before 1869, it was not possible for passengers to communicate with the guard if they had a problem, and it was not until the 1890s that they could walk from one compartment to another along a corridor. The corridor walkway becomes more common after the early 1900s when lavatories started to be introduced on trains.

The isolation of the railway carriage makes it the perfect scene for crimes of theft and assault, and even murder. In 1864, Thomas Briggs, a 69-year-old banker, was beaten and robbed while travelling by train, and his body was thrown from the compartment. He was the first person to be murdered on an English railway; a German tailor named Franz Müller was convicted of the crime and hanged.

Railway carriages are also ideal for blackmailers. With no witnesses to an incident, it will be your word against the other person, and if it is a woman, she will usually be believed. For this reason, avoid compartments with a single occupant of either sex. Max O'Rell warned readers of *John Bull and His Island*:

'If you value your reputation in the least, never remain alone in a compartment with a woman...There are certain ladies in existence who levy black mail on a vast and somewhat fantastic scale. A French diplomatist of my acquaintance was one day travelling alone with a woman, who appeared to him to be a lady in every respect. At the end of about half an hour, their eyes chanced to meet. The lady immediately smiled...My friend smiled too. Nothing more. But he paid for it. When just five minutes from Cannon Street Station, the lady threatened to tell staff at the station that he had insulted her, unless he paid her twenty pounds immediately. He paid.'

Once you've chosen your compartment, put your carpet bag underneath the seat opposite the one in which you are sitting. If you need to get off the train temporarily, perhaps to buy some refreshments or a newspaper, you can secure your place by leaving a personal article such as an umbrella, glove or book on the seat. Bear in mind that although smoking was strictly prohibited, even with the consent of the passengers, it was still common for gentlemen to light up their cigars, making the compartment stink of tobacco within seconds.

Standard etiquette dictated that the person seated nearest the window, normally the one facing the engine, could decide whether to have the window open or shut. In *Hints to Lady Travellers* (1889), Lillias Campbell Davidson stressed that only light items of luggage should be placed in the nets above the heads of passengers:

> *'I know a lady who narrowly escaped a broken neck by her husband's portmanteau falling upon her head from the luggage-rack above, and I should advise all my lady readers to put their own weighty encumbrances under the seat, and to make sure that they are not seated beneath anyone else's ponderous possessions.'*

If you visit Victorian England after 1875, you'll notice some changes on the railways. In that year, the Midland Railway abolished second-class travel and upgraded third-class passengers to second-class standards. It also reduced the fares in first-class. Other railways followed suit to keep up with the competition. The Midland Railway was also the first to introduce the Pullman car to British railways in 1874, with two experimental sleeping cars. The company realised the potential the Pullman could offer for luxurious comfort on trains to holiday resorts and in 1875, a Pullman parlour car was used on an express train from London Victoria to Brighton.

Although accidents did happen, you can expect your journey to be comparatively safe. Most injuries to passengers happened as a result of them trying to alight or board a train while it was still in motion. In 1859, John Davis, a chimney sweep from Oldbury, attempted to jump out of a carriage at New Street Railway Station in Birmingham while it was moving. According to the *Birmingham Daily Post*, he slipped and fell, severely fracturing his left thigh and sustaining a compound fracture of the left knee. His left thigh was amputated, but he died the following morning from the effects of the injury.

In cases of railway accidents, Lillias Campbell Davidson advised, 'at the first warning of a crash or violent swaying of the train, put your feet upon the opposite seat' as 'carriages, in a collision, 'telescope', and the seats are often driven together with great violence'. She does not explain how to do this if the seat was occupied by another passenger.

When you reach your destination, you will find an army of porters ready to help with your luggage. Although it was expressly forbidden to pay tips to railway porters under the by-laws, the practice was universal. In Lillias Campbell Davidson's opinion, porters were 'an underpaid and overworked class, and almost invariably civil, attentive and obliging'. Female attendants were also at every terminus and refreshment station to look after and wait on ladies and children.

Riding on an Omnibus

If you visit any large Victorian town, you will have the opportunity to ride on a horse-drawn omnibus. This was the preferred public transport of the middle-classes since it was cheaper than travelling by cab. Max Schlesinger observed that 'among the middle classes of London, the omnibus stands immediately after air, tea and flannel in the list of necessaries of life'. In country districts, the omnibus is an important link between places with no branch railway line and the main railway station for the area. They are timetabled to meet the trains, but omnibuses are largely an urban phenomenon.

The first omnibus service in England is believed to have been started in 1824 by John Greenwood, who operated between Salford and Manchester. This no-frills vehicle was 'little more than a box on wheels'. Although short journey stagecoaches were not new, the omnibus plied for hire along its route, picking up and setting down passengers along the way. There was no need to book a seat or to wait very long for a 'bus to come along.

In London, the omnibus service was established between Marylebone Street and the Bank of England via King's Cross in 1829. Omnibuses were drawn by a pair of horses and staffed by a driver and a conductor. Molly Hughes recalled the London horse-buses of the 1870s in which she travelled with her mother when they went for a morning's shopping:

'I reckon that the journey from Islington to the West End took a good deal over an hour. Wedged as we were, it was impossible to see anything out of the tiny windows, and

the journey was sheer boredom. What with the lack of air, the jerks of the frequent stops, and the jolting over the stone-paved roads, I was usually too ill to stay the course, and we had to get out some distance before our required shop.'

Inside an omnibus, you will find straw on the floor to keep the feet of passengers warm and dry. By the end of the day, this will be wet and dirty. The straw also harbours fleas when dry and the ague when wet. The interior of the omnibus is notoriously stuffy and poorly ventilated, with no air except when the door is opened. Blue velvet covers the seats, but any luxury implied by this material will quickly be forgotten once you sit down. You will be tightly wedged in beside the other passengers, and you will feel a painful jolt every time the 'bus stops. Your toes will be crushed when people get on and off the omnibus, and you will invariably have sticks or parasols poked into your chest or neck. Add in the steam of damp umbrellas, the cries of squalling babies, and the hazard of pickpockets and sickly passengers sitting next to you, and you have the journey from hell.

In 1866, the *Penny Illustrated Paper* complained about London's omnibuses, describing them as 'ill-ventilated, foul-strawed, close, and narrow boxes, contrived to carry eight and made to carry twelve'. More spacious buses from Manchester and Glasgow had been trialled but were too unwieldy for London streets. The paper went on to argue: 'It is pretty obvious that one great reason for all the failures is the practice of carrying too many passengers. In this way the roof ventilation is impeded by the legs of those who ride on the knife-board and impart a flavour of corduroy and damp blucher to the internal atmosphere. The space devoted to each person is (to say nothing of crinoline) absurdly insufficient'.

The best seat inside an omnibus depends on the time of year and how far you are travelling. Never take the seat by the door unless there is no other space or you are only going a few stops. If you do, you will be disturbed every time another passenger boards or alights, and you are very likely to get your fingers jammed or your clothing ripped in the door. If you're going the whole length of the journey, follow the advice of *The Magazine of Domestic Economy,* which wisely suggested choosing a seat in 'the farthest corner in winter, and within two of the end in summer, so as to have the benefit of the air'. When joining an omnibus which already had several passengers, another tip was to 'take your seat on that side which has the smallest number of stout persons'.

You may do better sitting on the knifeboard of the omnibus, located on the roof. There were tiny ledges on which to step to reach the 'knifeboard', a raised partition along the middle with seats on each side. Few women ventured there as it was so difficult to get on and off wearing a cumbersome skirt or crinoline. One of the conductor's duties in the crinoline age was to 'lean down from his perch and prevent with his hand the oval that hoops or whalebone had to assume when squeezing through the narrow doorway from rising to an indelicate height as they were somewhat prone to do', recalls Alfred Rosling Bennett in *London and Londoners in the 1850s & 1860s* (1924).

The knifeboard design was replaced by the 'garden seat' omnibus in the 1880s, which had a curved staircase at the rear leading to the top deck. This had a central gangway, benches facing the way the passengers were going, and 'decency' or 'modesty' boards on the top deck, which afforded some protection to the passengers, and prevented people passing from seeing the ladies' ankles. On the lighter garden seat omnibuses, there were often two seats either side of the driver. According to the granddaughter of a 'bus pioneer, they were 'much coveted by business men who travelled daily to work. They used to book their seats, tipping the conductor to reserve them. Some even had their own rugs'.

You will be able to identify your regular omnibuses by the bright colours in which they are painted. As you're a stranger, if you have a choice of several omnibuses and you're in a hurry, opt for one which has the most distant destination as they will travel quicker and will not ply for custom at the corner of every street. The American tourist David W. Bartlett warned readers of *What I Saw in London* (1853) that omnibus conductors 'have a wretched way of abbreviating the names of the places to which they drive, so that a stranger finds it impossible to understand them'. It could mean a lengthy delay in getting to your destination if you misunderstand or mishear the route.

Just before you reach the street opposite where you want to get off, ask the person by the door to tell the conductor to stop. On leaving the omnibus, you should hand your fare to the conductor, but not until you've alighted. In many omnibuses, the fares are marked up inside but if they are not, you should ask the fare for the journey you wish to make. In London particularly, the prices between four and half-past four were often doubled as that was when the City men left their offices for the day. Tickets were not introduced until 1891.

Taking a hackney-carriage

Another form of public transport you could try is the hackney-carriage, which was any wheeled carriage licensed to carry passengers. You can recognise them by the number on the back, and you'll see a variety of these vehicles on Victorian streets. Try a brougham first; they are enclosed four-wheeled carriages drawn by one horse which can seat two people. Sometimes there is a pair of fold-away seats at the front corners to seat a further two passengers. You will be able to see out through the glass front. Often used as private carriages and sold off by the gentry for a second lease of life, you may spot faded coats of arms on the exteriors.

If you've got lots of luggage, you'd better try a clarence. This is a larger version of the brougham which can seat four passengers, and is therefore popular with families travelling to and from railway stations. Drawn by two horses, it's four-wheeled and is glass-fronted. The clarence is known colloquially as a 'growler' because of the deafening noise it makes when driven over cobblestones or macadam roads. It's not the most comfortable vehicle either, with peeling paint, dirty straw and rattling windows.

Molly Hughes referred to the 'growlers' of the 1870s as being 'like the omnibuses, with the same dingy blue velvet, only much dirtier, and as they were used for taking people to hospitals my father used to call them "damned fever-boxes".' When the family needed to get to the station, 'luggage was piled on the top, and we were packed in among rugs, umbrellas, and hand-bags. At last the cabby climbed up to his seat and whipped his horse. It took an hour or more to jog along from Canonbury to Paddington'.

If you're in a crowded city and need to get somewhere fast, a cabriolet (or cab for short) is your best bet. Originally invented by Joseph Hansom in 1834 and refined by John Chapman two years later, it has two wheels and is pulled by one horse, making it very light and quick for steering around traffic jams. The driver sits on a raised seat behind and above the passengers' compartment with the horse's reins going over the top of it. You can communicate and pay him through the trap-door in the roof. Don't even think about dodging the fare as the cabman controls the doors by means of a lever, and can insist you pay before leaving the vehicle. Women quickly find that one of the problems with Hansom cabs is that the overhanging reins can knock off their hats, and dresses can easily be soiled on the rim of the wheel. It's also extremely difficult to get in and out of a Hansom with any dignity while wearing a crinoline.

Cabbies ply their trade from cab-stands only, not while moving. When getting into a cab, it's always wise to establish the distance you want to travel with the cabman (and therefore the fare) before it leaves. There may be an extra charge if you have any packages which must go outside the cab. If there's any dispute about the distance, you can insist that the cabman drive you to the nearest police office where you can make a deposit for the measurement of the ground. With regard to tipping,

Lillias Campbell Davidson suggested 'adding a copper or two to the fare, with the remark that it is for himself' as well as a stray newspaper.

Despite their speed, London cabs are not generally well-liked. Max Schlesinger wrote that the 'many crevices…let in wind and dust; the seats feel as if they were stuffed with broken stones; the check-string is always broken; the door won't shut; or if shut, it won't open; …to discover the faults of a London cab is easy'. By contrast, in the countryside, cabs are known as 'flies', and are considered very comfortable.

OTHER FORMS OF PUBLIC TRANSPORT

For the working classes, there was no affordable public transport until the arrival of trams, so they had to live within walking distance of their workplace. You may be surprised by the huge numbers of people walking around in Victorian England, whatever the weather.

If you're travelling on a budget, you'll find that trams are considerably cheaper than omnibuses. Originally horse-drawn, the first was introduced in Birkenhead in 1860. The network expanded in the 1870s, particularly in provincial cities such as Middlesbrough, where there were horse trams along the main routes from 1876. Electric versions first appeared in the 1890s. You could also take a trip on a pleasure steamer at any of the major ports such as London or Liverpool, or at a seaside resort.

If you're visiting London after 1863, you could try travelling on the Metropolitan Railway (the London Underground). Opened on 10 January, it's very popular with the public and is essentially the same as the conventional above-ground version, using steam engines with large airy stations. By the 1890s, it was possible to bore deeper under the city and the highly successful Central London Railway (the 'Tuppenny Tube') was opened in 1900 with electric locomotives.

The bicycle revolutionises travel for both sexes, especially for the middle and working classes, offering independence and new leisure opportunities. If you have a good sense of balance, you could attempt to ride one of the penny farthings which appear in 1870. For an easier ride, try a 'safety' bicycle which is popular from the 1880s. Once second-hand models became readily available, they were a real boon for people like domestic servants who could make the most of their weekly afternoons off by cycling to see friends and family.

Bicycles were also useful in rural areas which were not part of the railway network or even on a stagecoach or omnibus route. There really was little choice when it came to transport in these places. 'Carrier carts trundling two or three times a week between market towns and the villages were the only public transport (private enterprise), carrying papers, paraffin, parcels, poultry, and people', comments Leslie Baily.

In the late 1890s, motor-buses and motor-cars started to be seen on Victorian streets. At this time, they were still very much a novelty. However, in November 1896, 33 cars set out for Brighton from London as a celebration of the freeing of motor-vehicles from a speed limit of four miles per hour (it was increased to 12), and from the legal necessity to be preceded by a man carrying a red flag. This was the beginning of the trend for motorised transport, which gathered pace during the Edwardian era. It sounded the death-knell for the horse-drawn vehicles which had dominated Victorian England, and changed both the look and smell of the streets forever.

With your new knowledge of public transport, you're savvy enough to get out and about without fear of an accident. Next, why not indulge in a spot of shopping and search out unusual souvenirs to bring home for family and friends.

Changing Transport. *(Illustrated London News, 1897)*

NEW OMNIBUS REGULATION.

"'Werry sorry'm, but yer'l 'av to leave yer Krinerline outside."

(Above) Advertisement for the Y & N diagonal seam corset. *(Black and White, 1899)*
(Below) New Omnibus Regulation. *(Punch, 1858)*

Spring Fashions. *(Cassell's Family Magazine, 1885)*

Advertisement for Chas Baker & Co. Stores. *(Illustrated London News, 1887)*

North Country Mails at the Peacock Islington, 1838.
(Courtesy of Print & Photographs Division, Library of Congress, LC-DIG-pga-03502)

COUNTY HOTEL, LANCASTER.

JOSIAH S. DUCKSBURY
PROPRIETOR

(Above) A Crowded Crossing, from *London Pictures: Drawn with Pen and Pencil*, 1890.
(Below) The County Hotel, Lancaster, circa 1900.

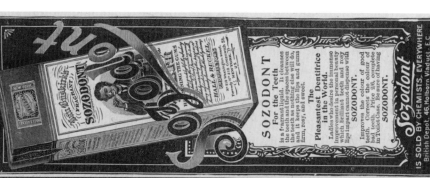

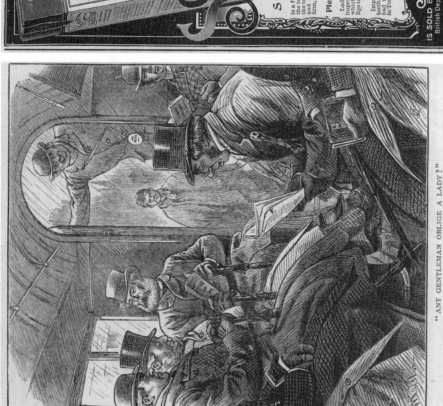

"ANY GENTLEMAN OBLIGE A LADY?"

(*Left*) 'Anyone Oblige a Lady?' (*Cassell's Family Magazine*, 1885)
(*Right*) Advertisement for Sozodont. (*Illustrated London News*, 1897)

(Left) Advertisement for Beecham's Pills. *(Illustrated London News, 1888)*
(Right) The Great Lozenge-Maker. *(Punch, 1858)*

A London Fair – Friday at the Metropolitan Cattle Market. (*The Graphic, 1892*)

A London May Day. (*The Graphic*, 1876)

(*Above*) 'What's Left', or Crumbs from the Rich Man's Table: Sketch Outside a Fishmonger and Poulterer's Shop. (*Illustrated London News, 1889*)
(*Below*) Between the Courses, from *Living London, 1901*.

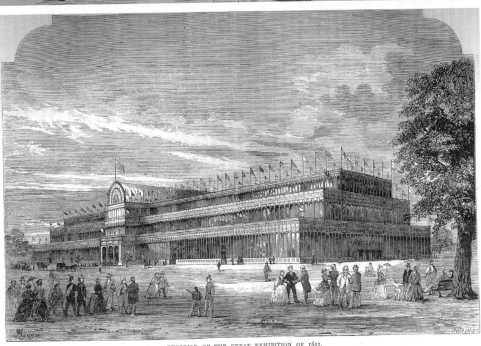

EXTERIOR OF THE GREAT EXHIBITION OF 1851.

(Above) Notes at a London Hospital: Saturday Night. *(The Graphic, 1879)*
(Below) Exterior of the Great Exhibition, 1851, from *Old and New London*, 1878. *(With thanks to Sue Wilkes)*

(*Left*) The new Great Western Arcade, Birmingham. *(Illustrated London News, 1876)*
(*Right*) Table D'hôte at the Trocadero, from *Living London, 1901.*

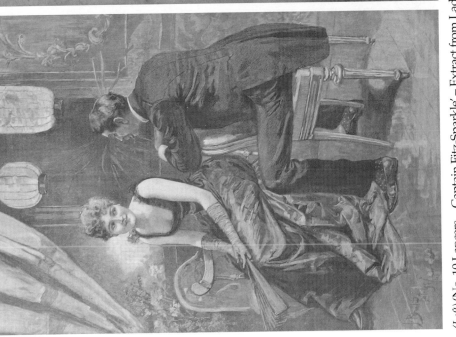

(*Left*) 'No. 10 Lancers...Captain Fitz-Sparkle' – Extract from Lady Maude's Dance Programme. (*The Illustrated London News, Christmas Number 1892*)

(*Right*) *Carte de visite* of a couple with their baby, circa 1880.

(*Above*) London Sketches: At A Music Hall. (*The Graphic, 1873*)
(*Below*) Scarborough Sands from Fish Pier, circa 1900.

(*Above*) London Sketches: A Country Visitor. (*The Graphic, 1873*)
(*Below*) Inside a Public House on a Saturday Night from *Living London, 1901.*

Christmas Morning: Three Generations. *(The Illustrated London News, Christmas Number 1883)*

Chapter Six
Shopping

'Behold Regent Street at two p.m...Not without reason do I declare it the most fashionable street in the world...Regent Street is an avenue of superfluities – a great trunk road in Vanity Fair. Fancy watchmakers, haberdashers, and photographers; fancy stationers, fancy hosiers, and fancy staymakers; music shops, shawl shops, jewellers, French glove shops, perfumery, and point lace shops, confectioners and milliners.'
(George Augustus Sala, *Twice Round the Clock,* **1859)**

From markets, bazaars and village shops through to co-operatives, specialist retailers and department stores, in Victorian England you can buy an amazing cornucopia of goods for both the necessities and luxuries of life. In towns, the type of shops you will come across depends largely on whether you're exploring a working-class district or a more affluent area. In the poorest streets, where the people have little or no spare money, all you will find are gin palaces, pawnbrokers, cook-shops, rag-and-bottle stores and chandlers' shops (selling small quantities of cheese, bacon and groceries). Small market towns have a good variety of stores, while in a rural village, there is usually just one shop stocking anything and everything.

MONEY, MONEY, MONEY

All the main types of shops – the grocer, the baker, the fishmonger and so on – offer small amounts of credit to their customers. Transactions are recorded in a book, sometimes called a 'trust book', and the account has to be paid at the end of the week before more goods can be bought on 'trust' for the next week. To buy 'on tick' or 'on the slate' is a common practice in working-class areas where the main breadwinner is paid weekly. Of course, problems arise when the customer is unemployed or cannot work through illness, and falls behind with payments. There comes a point when the shopkeeper can no longer extend credit, and at this stage, the poor turn to pawnbrokers and chandlers' shops. When all avenues to obtain money to buy food have been exhausted, families have little choice but to seek admission to the workhouse.

The credit system is also used at the opposite end of the social scale. Middle and upper-class customers have accounts set up with the shops they regularly buy from, which are settled weekly, monthly or even quarterly. One advantage of this is that servants can be sent to buy goods without the need for them to carry money, avoiding the risk of them being tempted to steal it or falling prey to pickpockets.

As you are a stranger in Victorian England, it's unlikely that you will be able to obtain credit from shops, so you will need to pay for everything in cash. Only the wealthy have bank accounts and access to cheques; everyone else is paid in, and uses, cash in the form of coins (rarely notes) as part of daily life. Victorian currency consists of lots of different coins in circulation. Goods are priced and sold in pounds, shillings and pence, or written as £, s and d. Costs are not always expressed using these symbols; in fact, it is more common to see prices like 2/6, which stands for two shillings and sixpence.

SERVICE WITH A SMILE

You may not recognise some of the smaller establishments as shops at all. Many shopkeepers serve customers through an open window at the front of the premises; you remain on the street and do not actually go into the shop. Some larger establishments also operate in this way or by using a trestle table in the street, as well as trading inside. This provides a better chance of capturing passing customers. These shops are not very hygienic, especially if they are selling food, as flies can easily settle on the produce.

When you enter a larger Victorian shop, the first thing you will probably notice is that customers are served from the counter, unlike modern self-service stores. The staff will treat you with deference, especially if it appears that you have money to spend. Shopkeepers work hard to retain custom, and to loyal shoppers with an account, they offer a home delivery service. This is provided by more and more shops in the 1880s and 1890s when the bicycle comes into common use and boys are employed specifically to deliver goods to customers at home.

Although you'll pay at the counter, few small shops have a till or cash register before the late nineteenth century. They use a wooden cash tray with bowls for the coins, or a simple drawer instead. If you visit a large draper's, co-operative or department store in the early 1880s, look out for a new invention: the overhead 'cash railway' which originated as Lamson's Cash Balls. This is a system in which money and bills are placed in hollow capsules, and transported on an overhead wire to a central cash office by means of a pulley operated by the counter assistant; the change comes back the same way. The system is designed to eliminate errors or fraud, but it also provides endless amusement to bored children out shopping with their parents.

You'll also notice that shops stay open late into the night, for six days a week, sometimes seven. This is particularly the case in working-class districts, where evening trade is so important; retailers selling food stay open until midnight, and often later on Fridays and Saturdays. Although this is convenient for customers, it means that working conditions for staff are very difficult. In more affluent areas such as the West End of London or other large cities like Manchester, Birmingham or Liverpool, shops usually close at six o'clock during the week, and some are only open for half the day on Saturdays after 1894.

Apprentices in shops worked even longer hours than the assistants. In 1881, H. G. Wells was appointed as an apprentice draper's assistant in the Southsea Drapery Emporium, which he loathed. He recalled working thirteen-hour days, from seven in the morning until eight at night, except on Wednesday (early closing day), when the shop shut at five. He wrote:

'We apprentices were roused from our beds...We flung on old suits...and were down in the shop in a quarter of an hour, to clean windows, unwrapper goods and fixtures, dust generally before eight'. A breakfast of bread and butter followed. Then:

'I had to fetch goods for the window dresser and arrange patterns or pieces of fabric on the brass line above the counter. Every day or so the costume window had to be rearranged and I had to go into the costume room and fetch those headless effigies on which costumes are displayed and carry them the length of the shop, to the window dresser, avoiding gas brackets, chairs and my fellow creatures en route. Then I had to see to the replenishing of the pin bowls and the smoothing out and stringing up of paper for small parcels.'

Wells remembered how the 'tediums of the day were broken for an hour or so' when he was sent out on errands to get lengths of material or ribbon from other shops, or take bags of change to the bank. Back at the drapers,

'there were a hundred small fussy things to do, straightening up, putting away, fetching and carrying. It was not excessively laborious but it was indescribably tedious...And as soon as the doors were shut and the last customer gone, the assistants departed and we junior apprentices rushed from behind the counters, scattered wet sawdust out of pails over the floor and swept it up again with great zest and speed, the last rite of the day'.

THE POWER OF ADVERTISING

Shops and places of entertainment have to use ingenious means to attract custom and beat the competition. Some resort to 'sandwich-men' who crowd the streets, wedged fast between two heavy placarded boards. According to *Chambers's Journal* (1850), 'These poor fellows, whose bread, sandwiches as they are, can hardly be said to be well buttered, receive invariably a shilling a day for carrying their Sinbad load, from which they are only released when it becomes too dark to read'. These walking advertisements are commonplace, but look out for more eye-catching versions.

Max O'Rell recalled walking in Fleet Street in *John Bull and His Island*: 'To my great astonishment, I saw pass a dozen fellows with shaved heads and dressed in convicts' uniform. They were accompanied by a warder...chained in couples, and on their backs a large '14' was visible. It was the advertisement of a vaudeville named 'Fourteen Days' and which was being played with success at the Criterion Theatre at the time'.

When you're exploring the fashionable streets of London or in another large city, see if you can spot the 'gazer' walking around. This is a man who has the appearance and manners of an aristocratic gentleman, but is actually employed by several different shops to generate interest in their goods. They rig him out in a fashionable outfit complete with a gold-headed cane or handsome umbrella, a neck-tie and handkerchief, and a gold watch, a showy ring and a handsome double eye-glass. *Chambers's Journal* notes that all the 'gazer' has to do is 'walk leisurely from the shop of one of his patrons to that of another, stopping in front of the window and scrutinising with much apparent interest and complacency the various objects displayed to public view. In so doing, he handles his gold eye-glass with aristocratic grace, drops a monosyllabic ejaculation of surprise or commendation, and when half-a-score of simpletons have gathered round to admire the astonishing cheapness and perfection of the wares, he pops into the shop, [and] gives an order in a loud and pompous tone for a dozen of the article which the tradesman wants to push off'. He then walks on to the next shop to repeat the process. His pay varies from half-a-crown to three-and-sixpence a day, 'according to his figure and effrontery'.

The female version of the 'gazer' has a more dowdy appearance. She stands in the doorway of shops such as milliners to capture indecisive customers and encourage them to go inside. The *Chambers's Journal* comments that 'she is to the shopkeeper what the landing-net is to the angler; it is her office at the precise crisis between hesitation and resolve, to lug the half-unwilling victim who has bitten the tawdry bait, into the interior of the shop, where she is handed over to persons too well skilled in the art of perpetrating a sale to leave her any chance of escape'.

If you are a woman shopping alone, you would do well to follow the advice of 'An Old Stager', particularly in London:

'Strange shops should be entered with caution. There are handsomely set-out ones − in the best streets, too − where, if they got a lady in alone, they will try to bully her into buying, and cheat her most desperately into the bargain. As a general rule, where the shopmen are extremely urgent and importunate, insisting upon showing things instead of answering your question

*about price, make up your mind that they are cheats,
and get out of the shop as quick as you can'.*

THE DAILY GROCERY SHOP

Without refrigeration or freezers, perishable foodstuffs
like milk, butter, eggs and meat cannot be kept fresh
for very long. Large country houses have their own
ice houses and the rich have lead-lined ice-boxes in
their town-house cellars, but the humble middle-class
working man has only a cool larder to keep his food
in. Although refrigerators are exhibited at the Great
Exhibition in 1851, they are large and cumbersome, and
not suitable for home use. Not until the twentieth century
will the ordinary family have access to refrigeration.

As a result, shopping for food has to be done at least
every couple of days, if not every day. The average middle-
class consumer shops at a bakery for bread, a butcher's for
meat, a grocer's for dry goods such as sugar, tea, coffee
and rice, and dairy shops for milk, butter, eggs, cream
and cheese. Early shops have wooden countertops and
floors, which are difficult to keep free of dirt. In the late
nineteenth century, the importance of food hygiene is
taken more seriously, and marble counters and tiled walls
are introduced which are far easier to clean. In Victorian
food shops, people buy smaller quantities of foodstuffs and
simply ask for the weight they require. This is measured
out and wrapped in paper by the smartly-dressed shop
staff. Liquids are often measured into the customers' own
jugs, especially in working-class districts.

From about the 1870s, cheap imports of meat, fish and fruit from overseas lead to an improvement in diet for those who can afford it, but do not affect the working and lower working classes. Many of them have to shop for food at the end of the day, when the leftovers are marked down in price. The diet of the wealthy is the most varied and might include exotic fruits such as peaches, pineapples and grapes as well as shellfish, meat, poultry and game.

To be successful, tradesmen have to offer a wide range of goods and services. In 1873, William Benson advertises his business in Malvern Wells as 'Confectioner, Fancy Bread & Biscuit Baker and Dealer in British Wines'. He can provide 'Rich Wedding and other Cakes on the shortest notice' and supplies families with 'genuine home-made bread daily'. Yet, this is not the sum total of William Benson's services. He also describes himself as 'Corn Factor and Provision Merchant', 'Agent for the General Fire and Life Insurance Office' and 'Family Grocer, Tea Dealer and Italian Warehouseman'. William Benson also offers home-cured hams and bacon, and Huntley and Palmer's biscuits, and could secure apartments for families 'on the shortest notice'.

When John James Sainsbury advertised his 'High Class' provisions store at Croydon in 1894, he described some of his other outlets and the types of goods for sale:

'The shops are well lighted, and elegantly fitted with mahogany, the walls being lined with tesselated [sic] tiles, while marble slabs and counters give to the whole an inviting air of coolness and cleanliness at the hottest season. The [stock] is of the most comprehensive description, embracing the choicest butters of absolute

purity, obtained direct from the farms of Brittany, Dorset, and Aylesbury; new-laid eggs; Wiltshire and Irish bacon, York and Irish hams; the finest English, American, and Continental cheeses; ox-tongues in tins; fresh and salt dairy-fed pork; and all descriptions of poultry and game when in season.'

Sainsbury attributed the success of his store to good customer service and to the 'promptness and attention [and] the marked civility and alertness of one and all of [the] staff'. Customers could also have their purchases delivered, and deliveries were made by a large number of horses and carts. Ironically, John James Sainsbury started his first shop in the poor working-class districts of London, but spotted the potential for expansion with more upmarket premises and stock for middle-class customers. *(Reproduced by permission of The Sainsbury Archive, Museum of London Docklands).*

BARGAIN-HUNTING

Markets and street vendors are cheaper than shops, which have higher overheads, and so they are popular with the working classes. You're more likely to find a bargain at an indoor or outdoor market than anywhere else, as goods are often second-hand and you can haggle if you're brave enough. The lifeblood of working-class districts, you can buy almost anything at a market from meat, fish and fruit and vegetables to old clothes, candles and furniture. Large cities have more than one market, usually specialising in a particular commodity.

According to *Cornish's Guide to Birmingham* (1858), the chief market hall can accommodate 600 stalls:

'Fruit-shops, similar to those in the centre avenue of Covent Garden Market, and game and poultry-shops, have been erected on either side of the chief entrances. There are also twelve butchers' shops, and eighteen fish-stalls in the centre of the Hall; and each of these stalls, as well as the fish and game shops, are fitted with a water-tap, and an independent drain to each, preventing escape into the Hall of any offensive effluvia.'

The wonderfully-named 'bazaar' is a type of shop with lots of different traders operating from one set of premises. They each rent a counter, and offer a wide variety of fancy goods like toys, haberdashery and jewellery. The proprietor of Noah's Ark Fancy Repository in Worcester Street, Kidderminster advertised his recently enlarged remodelled showroom in the *Gazetteer and Directory of Worcestershire* (1873). It contained 'the greatest variety of USEFUL and FANCY ARTICLES in Kidderminster, including Workboxes, Writing Desks, Croquet, Fishing Tackle, Jewellery and Electro Plated Goods, Rocking Horses, Toys, Combs, Brushes, Baskets &c'.

In most bazaars (and indeed, any high-class shop), the marked price is what you pay; bargaining is not allowed and you will find yourself red-faced with embarrassment if you try to do so. Signs warn the customers, 'Prices shall be marked on all the goods, from which no abatement shall be made'. However, a rather different type of bazaar, the Penny Bazaar, is started by Michael Marks in Leeds in 1884. These shops have open displays, similar to market stalls. They are popular because of the novelty that everything costs a penny, yet they still provide a wide variety of goods and there is no obligation to buy. Marks teamed up with Tom Spencer in 1894 to create Marks & Spencer.

All under one roof

Without a doubt, the development of department stores in the second half of the nineteenth century changed the face of shopping in large towns and cities in England. William Whiteley led the way when he opened his shop in Westbourne Grove in London in 1863. At first, he sold only ribbons, lace and fancy goods, but within five years he had 'expanded to include silks, linens, mantles, drapery, millinery, ladies' outfitting, furs, umbrellas and artificial flowers', according to Valerie Cumming in *Exploring Costume History*. During the 1870s, Whiteley was also offering 'groceries, meat, ironmongery, books, a house agency, outside catering, hairdressing, dry cleaning and a laundry service'. Whiteley's provided a home delivery service to London and the suburbs, and could dispatch goods to the provinces by train.

Similar shops open elsewhere in London and in other English cities and towns. Many of the new department stores recognise the need to offer restaurants and cloakrooms with lavatory facilities for their customers, particularly women. Nevertheless, they are not for everyone. Molly Hughes set up home with her husband in London and her memoir *A London Home in the 1890s* records her experiences:

> '*Bessie [her maid] advised me to get everything at Whiteley's. "You've only got to walk into the shop, order what you want in the different departments, and you find everything delivered at your door." She was right, but I soon found that this easy way of buying had to be paid for by too high prices, so I determined to explore the neighbourhood, buy what I wanted, and bring it home myself*'.

For the wealthy, shopping becomes a leisure pursuit in the last quarter of the nineteenth century. They are drawn to the new, well-lit department stores like moths to a flame. These shops, with their attractively arranged plate-glass window displays, originate in the USA. The Army & Navy Stores first opens in 1871 (begun as a co-operative society), and Liberty is founded in London in 1875.

Shirley Nicholson points out in *A Victorian Household* that Marion Sambourne used the Metropolitan Railway to reach her favourite shops after it was extended to South Kensington in 1868, with a convenient stop at Kensington High Street: 'Marion used it for going to Whiteley's in Westbourne Grove, to the Baker Street Bazaar, to Maples or Shoolbreds in Tottenham Court Road, or to Gamages at Holborn'. In addition, Harvey Nichols (Marion's favourite shop in Sloane Street) and Marshall and Snelgrove in Oxford Street were accessible by omnibus. Marion could easily reach Bakers and Pontings in Kensington High Street on foot.

'Poor but genteel girls' work as shop assistants

in these new stores, according to Suzanne Fagence Cooper in *The Victorian Woman*. She quotes from *The Girl of the Period Miscellany* (1869) which comments that a young lady working in a dress department was 'engaged…for certain qualifications of figure, in addition to educational acquirements. She must speak French (occasionally she understands German), and must, of course…be quick at arithmetic, and possessed of winning address, even temper and patience'.

CLOTHES-SHOPPING

Both men and women shop for new clothes when the seasons change, or for special occasions, such as attending a ball, a wedding or a funeral. In her diary spanning 1864-65, 23-year-old Adelaide Pountney frequently records shopping trips to purchase clothing or millinery items. The daughter of a deceased clergyman, Adelaide was usually accompanied by her sisters Louisa ('Louy') or Rose, or her mother ('Mamma').

On 10 May 1864 while living in Leamington, she wrote: 'Mamma, Louisa and I went out shopping. I bought a hat with a broad brim in spite of Louisa'. She added a drawing to the diary entry with the caption: 'Scene. Perry's shop. LP advising AMP to adopt the very becoming hat without any brim at all. AMP decides this time upon following her own instinct which tells her not to choose LP's favourite shape'. The previous day, all three had been out shopping and Louisa 'ordered a boot at Riches with a very deep military heel'. The sisters seem to have had very different opinions when it came to clothing, with the younger Louisa possibly being more fashion-conscious. In October 1864, Adelaide wrote: 'L bought some epaulettes for her dress'. These are ornamental shoulder pieces, which were very popular in the 1860s.

In April 1865, Adelaide wrote: 'We all went to Betts's to buy spring raiment as the burden of our linseys is greater than we can bear". Linsey is a thick, woollen fabric used in winter clothes, so perhaps summer came early in 1865. The 'spring raiment' bought by Adelaide and her family was probably not ready-made, but dress lengths to be made up by a dressmaker.

Shops specialising in all kinds of clothing build up a strong clientele in London and the large cities, and are often able to expand into spa towns. In *Shops and Shopping*, Alison Adburgham quotes from an advertisement placed in the *Cheltenham Chronicle* in 1844 by Debenham, Pooley & Smith (later Debenhams). With a shop in Wigmore Street, London and another in Harrogate, the company was announcing a new branch at Cavendish House on the Promenade, Cheltenham. It offers for sale:

'a Stock unrivalled in extent, and selected with the greatest care from the British and Foreign Markets, consisting of every novelty in SILKS, CACHMERES, SHAWLES, MANTELS, CLOAKS, LACE and EMBROIDERY; FLANNELS and BLANKETS; MOREEN, DAMASK and CHINTZ FURNITURE; SHEETINGS, DAMASK TABLECLOTHS, and Linen Drapery of every description; COBOURG AND ORLEANS CLOTHS; A Large Lot of French Merinoes, Exceedingly Cheap; READY-MADE LINEN, for Ladies and Gentlemen;

Baby Linen and Children's Dresses of every kind; also A CHOICE STOCK OF FURS FAMILY MOURNING. FUNERALS conducted in the most careful manner, at moderate charges.'

CASHING IN WITH 'DIVIS'

If you visit the north of England in the mid-nineteenth century, you can also try shopping at a co-operative store. These shops originate with the Rochdale Pioneers in 1844, but they all offer the unique incentive of quarterly cash dividends on purchases for all members. By the time of Queen Victoria's death, 'nearly one third of all societies paid dividends between 3s and 4s in the pound, the equivalent of up to a 20 per cent price reduction', comments Michael J. Winstanley in *The Shopkeeper's World*. You won't benefit from the 'divis' because they reward loyalty over a long period of time, but the high dividend rate attracts and retains customers.

By 1881, the stores are still predominantly in the north with more than 547,000 members. In the early Edwardian period, the co-op starts to spread to other areas of England. At first, they concentrate on groceries and provisions, offering pure and unadulterated food at fixed, reasonable prices. Later, the co-op expands into men's and women's clothing, meat, milk, bread, and fruit and vegetables, as well as other household goods. In effect, it becomes a mini-department store.

In many ways, the village shop is the most fascinating of all. Here, you can eavesdrop on the latest gossip and peruse an extraordinary variety of goods. In *The New Monthly Belle Assemblée* (1848), Clara Payne describes a typical village shop:

> '*Numerous green hard-looking apples are placed in a row before the basket and a variety of pale little currant cakes are stuck against the pane of glass, supported by battledores and shuttlecocks, while gorgeously painted kites occupy the rear; with hoops, and bats, and various toys for girls and boys. Implements of industry are everywhere visible – balls of cottons, pins, needles, tapes, twine, shoe binding, hooks and eyes, thimbles and buttons, slate pencils and lead pencils, paper and ink, wafers and wax, quills and pens, are all in this little shop met together; with mops and brooms, bricks and brushes, pepper and salt, tobacco and tea, candles and soap, flour and snuff, sugar and spice, and all that is nice.*'

The *Chambers's Journal of Popular Literature, Science and Arts* (1861) goes further. The village shop 'answers to the Oriental bazaar in being at once the great reservoir and exchange of parochial gossip, and the place where everything can be bought, and where, in default of other marts, everything must be bought. The shop contains all wares, from a reel of cotton to a pound of small-shot, and numbers among its customers everybody, from the esquire to the travelling tinker... its window is stored with bottles of raspberry drops, bulls' eyes and other coarse confectionery, tempting to children, with gingerbread, song-books, needles and tapes, Dartford gunpowder and Horniman's tea'.

In rural areas, itinerant traders, who tramp around an

area selling portable goods, remain an important part of the community. They appear at different times of the year, offering the types of goods they know are likely to be popular with customers who have bought before. Itinerant hawkers in the late nineteenth century were 'colourful characters with their baskets and bundles, the man who renewed the rims on wash tubs and cow buckets, another with oatcakes and crumpets, one with broom heads slung from his shoulders,' according to a contributor to Pat Barr's *I Remember*.

'And we always welcomed the man who brought real honey in a tin hat-box affair and measured it into the jar. There were pegs from the gypsy, tinware and drapery from the packman'. There were also the pedlars who bought rabbit skins, the man who brought 'big blocks of salt for storing until pig-killing time, when bacon and hams were put to cure on the great stone table in the cellar, a mole catcher, the cheap-jack, and hurdle and wattle-fence makers'.

The only problem in finding suitable souvenirs from your trip will be that there are too many fancy goods to choose from. If you get the opportunity, try to visit some of the smaller emporiums as well as the new department stores. This will give you a broader shopping experience, and will allow you to eavesdrop on a greater variety of customers from the different social classes.

But as you indulge in a little window-shopping and walk about the streets, remember that in Victorian England health and safety is almost non-existent!

Chapter Seven
Health Hazards

'I find that the unsewered streets are generally in a very bad condition...Without sewers there can be no efficient drainage, and without drainage privies become superficial, offensive dumb wells, cellars are liable to contain water, and the ground generally becomes saturated with filth, and conditions of a character very inimical to health prevail. I have long observed that disease is most rife in streets of this character.'
(Report of Alfred Hill, Medical Officer of Health for Birmingham, 1873)

One of the toughest challenges you will face during your trip is staying healthy. Potential accidents are around every corner and in the overcrowded conditions of industrial towns, infectious diseases are rife while simple illnesses like diarrhoea kill thousands of babies each year. You will encounter a variety of memorable odours in Victorian England, and very few will be pleasant. Many are caused by poor sanitation, such as the 'noxious stenches arising through the grates in the street drains' described at East Retford, Nottinghamshire in 1849. At first, these strong smells will be difficult to get used to, so if you find them too overpowering, simply cover your nose with a handkerchief.

KEEPING CLEAN

The lack of clean water is probably the first thing you'll notice in Victorian England. Most people do not have a piped water supply into their homes, and must get their water from a standpipe or well in the street; this is frequently polluted. Even wealthy homes with water pipes only have them laid in the basement areas, and the supply is notoriously intermittent. Whether you're staying in a hotel, boarding-house, apartment or a better-class lodging house, it will be your chambermaid who provides the water for you to wash and bathe. She will bring you clean water for the bowl on your washstand, used for everyday washing. With this, you can have a wash-down using carbolic soap or soda.

If you want a hot bath, the water must be heated in a 'copper' in the scullery; this is a large copper-lined stove in which water is heated by lighting a pile of wood underneath. It is then brought up numerous flights of stairs to your room; when you've finished, the chambermaid will also remove the dirty water. Servants are the unsung heroes of Victorian society and without them, middle- and upper-class people would not be able to get a hot bath. Make sure you tip your chambermaid generously!

For the working classes, a weekly ritual is putting the family's tin bath in front of the fire downstairs. Starting with the head of the household, each member takes his or her turn to bathe using the same water; the last one is left with cold, grey water. Clothes are also washed in the 'copper' which, in poorer districts, is communal for each block or court of houses; it's usually located in an outhouse or brewhouse. The 'big wash' is traditionally done on Mondays and products such as Sunlight soap are routinely used when scrubbing the clothes.

If you fancy a proper bath, you could try going to the local bath-house. From the mid-1840s, an increasing number of public baths, many with laundries attached, are established in large towns across England. Huge numbers of people take advantage of them and when Coventry's new baths open in 1852, there are 'upwards of 1,000 bathers on the day of opening'. It's debatable whether the 'great unwashed' can afford to use the facilities which cost 1d for the plunge bath, and 2d for a warm private bath with the use of a towel. They are, however, affordable for those in employment and *The Graphic* points out that 'at the cost of a pint of the commonest beer the working man may enjoy an invigorating swim or a wholesome cleansing in a private warm bath'.

Bath-houses are split into separate areas for men and women. On both sides, there are baths with private facilities, plunging baths and swimming baths; all have first and second class options. The laundry section includes cleaning, drying and ironing facilities. This must seem like pure luxury to women living in crowded courts or alleys with only a communal brewhouse to wash in and nowhere in wet or cold weather to dry clothes, except the rooms in which they live. That's another reason for the smell of unwashed clothes you'll encounter everywhere you go, from the railways and omnibuses through to shops, theatres and lodgings.

Spending a penny

Perhaps the most obvious evidence of insanitary conditions you will spot is the lack of proper water closets. Despite this, the most popular designs originated in the eighteenth century. In 1775, Alexander Cumming had patented 'A Water Closet upon a New Construction' with water supplied by an overhead cistern, and a soil pipe with a double bend which was kept filled with water. The flush opened a sliding valve to let the water and its contents into the so-called 'stink trap'. Unfortunately, the sliding valve was not very efficient, leading to nasty congestion. Joseph Bramah improved on Cumming's design with the hinged two-valve closet he patented in 1778. When flushed, the contents of the closet were emptied and the water was let in at the same time. These water closets were manufactured until the late 1880s. New patents in the Victorian period included Thomas Twyford's first vitreous china lavatory in 1885 and Thomas Crapper's valve and siphon design in 1891.

The rudimentary Victorian water and sewage system cannot yet cope with the demand that widespread introduction of water closets would entail. Although a brick drain runs under every Victorian house, it is only sometimes connected to the public sewer (if there is one); otherwise, it runs into a cesspool. From 1848, legislation is introduced so that every new house has to be built with access to a water closet or ash-pit privy.

Only in the top hotels frequented by the wealthy will you find indoor flushing water closets. In all other types of accommodation, the water closet or privy will be outside. You will, however, have the benefit of a chambermaid whose many duties include emptying your chamber pot regularly. You'll quickly discover that the privy is located outside most private houses, either immediately at the back or at the end of the garden. It has a number of different names, such as the boghouse, convenience, necessary place, little house, and petty and netty (in the north-east).

Some water closets receive a little water when the water-works pump it through at irregular and not very frequent intervals. Of course, this is completely ineffective and night-soil men are employed to clear cesspits, privies and blocked drains. Also known as 'gold-diggers', they arrive after dark to empty the privy-middens by shovelling out the waste into barrows, and then onto horse-drawn carts. They visit each street about once a week, and sprinkle carbolic powder on the roadway before they leave. You will be well-advised to keep your window shut if the night-soil men visit the street where you're staying; when the contents of the privies are disturbed, the smell is beyond description. In the morning, housewives are always up early to swill the area by the privy.

If you're brave enough to venture into any of the poorest working-class districts to test the toilet facilities, you'll find that instead of water closets, the outside privies are either earth or 'dry' closets, or a type of 'wet' closet. These 'wet' closets are positioned over a drain or cess-pit, over a pail, or a wet midden. In 1871, Manchester has more than 38,000 privy middens; by the mid-1880s, most have been replaced by pail-closets. In Nottingham, the city has 10,000 more pail-closets than water-closets as late as 1908.

Dr Hector Gavin records his observations of the housing in Bethnal Green in *Sanitary Ramblings* (1848). He wrote:

> 'The disgusting and abominable state of the open and common privies proves a source of much disease and domestic discomfort in another way; women and children find these places so repulsive that they avoid them, and retain, in their ill-ventilated rooms, their refuse; the utensils are seldom emptied on account of the trouble there occasioned; the air of the rooms...becomes most offensive, and deleterious, and the walls absorb the emanations, and render the abode permanently unhealthy.'

While walking the streets, you will also notice a lack of public conveniences. They are first introduced at the Great Exhibition in 1851, when plumber George Jennings installs his 'monkey closets' in the retiring rooms. They prove hugely popular and during the exhibition, 827,280 visitors pay a penny to use them. The price includes a clean seat, a towel, a comb and a shoe-shine. When the Crystal Palace is moved to Sydenham at the end of the Exhibition, the toilets are retained and the entrance fees generate £1,000 a year.

The very first public toilets in the streets are not so successful. They are opened in London in February 1852 at the instigation of the Society of Arts. Known as 'public waiting rooms', the ladies' is at 51 Bedford Street, Strand while the men's is at 95 Fleet Street; the cost to use the facilities is twopence. Despite extensive advertising in *The Times* and the distribution of 50,000 handbills, the experimental 'public waiting rooms' are not very popular. After three months, the entrance fee is reduced to one penny but by October, the rooms are closed.

George Jennings, the plumber whose water closets had been so successful at the Great Exhibition, was an enthusiastic campaigner for public toilets which he called 'Halting Stations'. By 1895, 36 British towns have public conveniences but there are very few for women. The first underground public toilets had opened ten years earlier outside the Royal Exchange. The development of department stores and tea shops with toilet facilities are a real boon to upper-class and upper middle-class ladies as without them, they have to cut short their outings and return home. Lower middle-class and working-class women simply find somewhere private to squat and urinate, for instance, behind the bushes in a park, as witnessed by Walter, the anonymous author of *My Secret Life* (1888), who had an obsession with female urination.

Of course, toilet paper as you know it does not exist. Introduced in the USA in 1857, Gayetty's Medicated Paper is the first commercially produced toilet paper. Although perforated paper on a roll was invented in the 1870s and a patent was taken out in England in the 1880s, it is more common to find toilet paper sold in boxes of flat, separated sheets. Toilet paper is not usually displayed in chemists; instead, it is sold under the counter. It's thought too embarrassing to say the word 'toilet' in a shop so women ask for 'curling papers' instead. You can also buy it in stationers and hairdressers. It's clearly a luxury product and the working classes make do with squares of newspaper instead of toilet paper.

Incidentally, if you're a woman, sanitary towels are not available until the early 1880s and even then, only the wealthy can afford them. If you don't have the cash, you will have to get by with rags – alternatively, plan your visit for a better time of the month!

AVOIDING INFECTIOUS DISEASES

Life-threatening diseases are no respecter of social class, so you could be affected whether you are mingling with the rich or poor. This is largely because until the mid-nineteenth century, there was a lack of understanding about how diseases are spread. You'll find that people constantly worry about their health and that of their family – for good reason. Epidemics of infectious diseases are an accepted part of everyday life and they come and go in seemingly never-ending cycles of typhus and typhoid, cholera, smallpox, measles and scarlet fever. By the 1880s, the major killers of society are respiratory diseases such as tuberculosis.

There may be a slightly lower risk of contracting an infectious disease if you're visiting the Victorian countryside. People in rural areas still endure poor living conditions in damp and dilapidated cottages, and they suffer from poverty and sickness. Yet, as the population density is not as high as in urban districts, this makes the countryside a comparatively better place to live.

Unlike the Victorians, you know how diseases are spread and can take steps to avoid them. For instance, both typhus and relapsing fever are transmitted through parasites such as ticks, fleas and lice. Carefully examining your clothing and bed to eliminate 'hitch-hikers' is essential, as is the liberal use of insect powder to kill any you find. Popular brands like Keating's and Bayly's can be bought from any corner chemist. If someone starts to cough and sneeze next to you in the street, on an omnibus or train, move away as fast as possible or cover your mouth and nose with a handkerchief. People afflicted with diphtheria, measles, smallpox and tuberculosis can easily pass on their infection through droplets transmitted when coughing or sneezing.

Avoid drinking water from public fountains or taps. In fact, hot drinks may be the best option as the water will at least be boiled. Both cholera and typhoid (also known as enteric fever) can be caught through drinking water contaminated by infected faeces; typhoid is also present in contaminated food. Also, steer clear of any accommodation where there has been a scarlet fever (also known as scarlatina) or erysipelas outbreak as they are both spread through contact with infected material such as clothing or bedding. Erysipelas can also be passed on through the coughing and sneezing of infected patients.

Potentially fatal accidents are around every corner and if you break a limb, you could be in serious trouble. Bone-setting is the relatively easy part; infection and shock are the major killers. Being taken to hospital before the 1870s can easily cause your demise, even if your original injuries are taken care of. Treating deadly infections successfully is one of the major medical discoveries of the Victorian period, along with the use of anaesthetics, so the safest time to visit is after 1880. There are some extremely dangerous Victorian occupations but going about your daily business can be just as hazardous. Being run over by a vehicle such as a cart or omnibus is a very real risk so you will need to take great care in the streets full of horse-drawn traffic.

Danger also lurks indoors. Be very careful when standing in front of an open fire or adding coal or wood to it; long dresses and shawls can easily catch fire and result in serious burns, or even death. Another risk is being scalded by hot water if you accidentally knock over a kettle or pot on an open fire. Drugs such as arsenic and opium are readily available and used at home, and accidental poisoning is common among the illiterate or those who fumble around for medication in candlelight. Drug manufacturers start to introduce specially-shaped poison bottles from the 1860s onwards in an attempt to solve this problem.

Visiting the outpatient department of the local general hospital will help you to see the kinds of accidents which befall the average Victorian. Found in every large town, they are run in a similar way to today's accident and emergency departments. Patients with minor injuries and complaints are dealt with and sent home, while those with more serious medical or surgical problems are admitted to a ward for more in-depth treatment and/or observation. In *The London*, A. E. Clark-Kennedy quotes from Frederick Treves, a former surgeon at The London Hospital who started working there in 1867. The types of emergencies which the staff might have to deal with include 'a child who has swallowed a halfpenny...a man ridden over in the street; a machine accident with strips of cotton shift, mangled flesh and trails of black grease; someone picked up in a lane with his throat cut; or a woman, dripping foul mud, who has just been dragged out of the river'.

ACCESSING MEDICAL TREATMENT

If you feel under the weather, your first port of call should be the local corner chemist's. These shops are easily identified by the huge coloured glass bottles in the window, in amber, green and blue. At night, when gaslight is placed behind the bottles, the appearance is quite striking. Dispensing chemists are the main providers of healthcare for working-class and lower middle-class people. When someone in the family falls ill, they turn to the receipt book (an archaic term for recipes) handed down from previous generations which contains traditional herbal remedies. These are used well into the twentieth century. For instance, it is believed that if brown paper is stuck to the chest, it will ward off colds and coughs; eating garden snails is reputed to be a successful treatment for tuberculosis; and mistletoe is said to cure whooping cough. Receipts can be made up at the chemist's.

You will not have a family receipt book but the dispensing chemists will have their own versions for remedies and treatments of all manner of maladies and diseases. They also sell patent medicines manufactured by the big brands of the day such as Boot's, Beecham's and Holloway's, and they can advise on dosage. From the 1860s onwards, you can also buy patent medicines at grocers and general stores. Alternatively, you could go and see the local apothecary. He is licensed to provide medical advice for a fee, as well as dispensing and selling medicines. Avoid quacks if you can, since in most cases, you will simply be throwing your money down the drain. They peddle their wares in the street and also by post.

Traditional herbal remedies are still extremely important to the working classes, and some patent medicines are based on the same principles. For example, the ubiquitous Holloway's Pills invented by Thomas Holloway are advertised as a cure-all for digestive problems and other complaints. Advertisements state they 'strengthen the stomach, and promote the healthy action of the liver, purifying the blood, cleansing the skin, bracing the nerves, and invigorating the system'. An ointment is also marketed. The pills are hugely successful, not just in Britain but across the Empire, and make Holloway a multi-millionaire. After his death, the pills are analysed and found to contain nothing more than aloe, saffron and myrrh.

Aloe is also a key ingredient in Beecham's Pills, along with ginger, which continued to be sold well into the twentieth century. Originally a farm worker, Thomas Beecham had an interest in herbalism and he marketed a laxative pill which was ideal for Victorians with poor diets and restrictive clothing. With the slogan 'worth a guinea a box', the pills are designed to keep the digestive system regular but also purport to cure other illnesses too. An 1860 advertisement declares they are for 'bilious and nervous disorders, wind and spasms at the stomach, sick headache, giddiness, fullness and swelling after meals, drowsiness, cold chills, flushings of heat, loss of appetite, shortness of breath, costiveness, disturbed sleep, frightful dreams, and all nervous and trembling sensations'.

If remedies from the chemist don't do the trick, you may need to consult the local doctor. Most towns have a 'medical district' where the most successful practitioners lived; a doctor's private practice is usually run from his own house unless he can afford separate consulting rooms. You should always seek out medical advice from a qualified practitioner if you can afford it. Despite the tightening-up of the medical profession from 1858, many doctors, particularly those who have been practising for decades, are set in their ways, and the advice and treatments they prescribe are often little better than the quacks.

In 1887, when Beatrix Potter was suffering from rheumatic fever in her knees, she was treated by Mr Mould 'in whom we do not believe'. She wrote in her journal: 'It is my belief the old gentleman has but two medicines. I had first the camphor, then both mixed (!), then the quinine alone'.

In fact, Victorian doctors have a wide range of drugs they can prescribe. If you have constipation, a laxative such as sulphur or castor oil should work wonders. Purgatives, like senna and Epsom salts (sulphate of magnesia) will have a more energetic effect on your bowels. Emetics are used to induce vomiting and are invaluable when treating cases of poisoning. Mustard and salt-and-water, ipecacuanha wine and white vitriol (sulphate of zinc) fall into this category. To improve the appetite and aid digestion, bitters such as gentian, calumba, quassia and hops are given, the latter often in the form of bitter beer.

If you visit Victorian England in the summer and are struck down suddenly by the dreaded 'summer diarrhoea', nine times out of ten you will be prescribed essence of camphor. For violent attacks of this condition, the dose given is from three to five drops every ten minutes or a quarter of an hour until the symptoms have lessened, and then every hour. Camphor can be taken with brandy, in milk or on sugar, and is proven to deal with this type of sudden diarrhoea.

Tonics are useful to 'brace up and give increased tone to the system'. An example would be prescribing iron to treat anaemia, but preparations of bark and quinine are also frequently used. For bronchitis and coughs, expectorants help to loosen phlegm and ease the chest. Common expectorants are carbonate of ammonia, squills, ipecacuanha and tar.

Narcotics and opiates induce sleep, and many can relieve pain at the same time. The most widely-used is probably opium, followed by chloral hydrate. Opium is routinely prescribed to relieve pain from common complaints such as rheumatism or neuralgia, especially in damp, marshland areas such as Norfolk and Lincolnshire. Opiates are also used on a huge scale to pacify babies and young children. Godfrey's Cordial, a mixture of opium, treacle and infusion of sassafras, is the most popular children's drug and in Coventry, some ten gallons are sold each week which was sufficient for 12,000 doses. Opium in this form kills more babies through starvation than overdose, as being kept in a constantly drugged state makes them disinclined to suckle milk.

When you visit a dispensing chemist or doctor, don't be surprised if you're prescribed cod liver oil. This is the mainstay of Victorian medicine as it's known to be beneficial to patients suffering from various illnesses such as consumption and other wasting diseases, scrofula, bronchitis, asthma, rickets, gout and rheumatism. *The Family Physician*, written by physicians and surgeons of the principal London hospitals, recommends that Kepler's Extract of Malt and Cod-liver Oil can be 'used with confidence' to treat these diseases, although it is thought best to take small doses at a time.

William Fletcher, a 20-year-old clerk from Bridgnorth, suffered with consumption. In his diary in August 1859, he records a visit to a Birmingham physician, who prescribes pills to increase his appetite and strengthen him, and advises him to take plenty of cod liver oil, porter and port wine.

If you need dental treatment, it's easy to find someone to extract a tooth. This service is provided by barbers, blacksmiths, travelling 'tooth-drawers' and other quacks. If you can afford it, a more comprehensive range of dental services is available including the treatment of gum diseases, scaling, fillings, dentures, tooth-whitening and transplants. Regulation of the dental profession begins in the late 1850s with better training, but it is not until 1878 that it becomes compulsory for qualified professionals to be registered; from this time onwards, unqualified people cannot call themselves 'dentists' or 'dental practitioners'.

Beatrix Potter went to the dentist for the first time in her life in April 1883, when she consulted Mr Cartwright at 12 Old Burlington Street. She wrote in her journal:

*'He stopped a little hole in one of my top left double
teeth. It was a simpler business than I expected. He had
a little instrument with a head about as big as a pin's
head, which he whirled round and round to get out the
bad, wiped it with cotton-wool and rammed in gold as
if he meant to push the tooth out through the top of
my head. He did not hurt me in the least, only he had
only just come in when we did, and his fingers tasted
muchly of kid glove'.*

By the end of the nineteenth century, there are huge
improvements in the health of the nation. This is the
era in which surgical operations could be carried out
painlessly for the first time and were increasingly
offered to give patients a better quality of life, the causes
of long-feared diseases like cholera and smallpox
were identified and conquered, antiseptic and aseptic
conditions became the norm in every hospital, and
sanitation was improved in every large town or city.

Now that you are aware of potential health hazards
in the streets, you can safely go out and do some
people-watching!

Chapter Eight
Encounters with the Opposite Sex

'Before mixing with ladies, take off the coat in which you have been smoking, and rinse your mouth, lest your breath should be tainted with the 'weed'. Onions affect the breath still more disagreeably: beware of the effects of them. As a snuff-taker, you cannot have too large a supply of clean pocket-handkerchiefs, as those covered with snuff are disgusting to the beholders. We need hardly caution you against the offensive habit of spitting, when in ladies' company.'
(Cassell's Handbook of Etiquette, 1860)

Courtship is a complicated affair and as you will observe, it differs considerably, depending on the social class of a Victorian couple. There is also a far greater formality in personal relationships between ordinary men and women than in modern times.

Walking down a typical suburban street towards a public park, you pass rows of three-storey villas with gleaming sash windows and iron railings outside. Steps lead down to the basement floor of each one, where the kitchen and cellars are situated. At the doorway of one kitchen, you notice a housemaid lingering, perhaps longer than necessary, to chat with the butcher's boy. Her mistress will not be pleased if she finds out the maid's been flirting, especially during working hours;

servants like her are not allowed 'followers'.

Entering the park, you follow the meandering serpentine path around an ornamental lake. Benches are dotted here and there in shaded spots and as you approach a large willow tree, you hear a flirtatious giggle. Around the corner is a young, probably middle-class, couple sitting on a bench holding hands. When they see you, they quickly move apart, and the gentleman looks slightly bashful. The giggle returns as soon as you've passed them. Holding hands in public is not the done thing in Victorian England, unless you are an engaged couple. They are probably 'walking out' (literally) but are not yet at the stage of an official, parent-approved, engagement.

Back in the fashionable shopping quarter of town, you spot an exquisitely dressed upper-class lady with an older woman, possibly her mother or aunt, staring intently in the window of a draper's emporium. A smart-looking, moustachioed gentleman approaches and doffs his top hat to them. They evidently know each other, but there is a slight hesitation before the young lady takes his arm and they continue walking along the street. The older woman does not leave their side; it is her role to act as chaperone to her unmarried daughter or niece on this unexpected meeting with a potential suitor.

COURTING COUPLES

When courting, a couple were said to 'walk out' together, to 'keep company' or to have an 'understanding'. For the upper and upper middle-classes, having a chaperone around unmarried couples was necessary to avoid any accusations of impropriety, and to ensure the chastity of the young lady. Rich gentlemen wanted their brides to be pure and innocent, so virginity was a valuable commodity in marriage negotiations.

A chaperone was essential at social gatherings where a young lady might meet eligible men. Ideally, the person tasked with the role would be a married woman 'possessing a large circle of acquaintances, who is popular as well as good-natured', according to *Manners and Rules of Good Society* (1888). At other less formal occasions, a girl could be chaperoned by an unmarried sister or cousin, or even by a brother. Gwen Raverat recalls the stringent rules relating to chaperones. Aged 35, her uncle Frank was engaged to his second wife Ellen, who was 27 and a Fellow and lecturer at Newnham College. When Miss Clough, the principal was away for a few weeks, Frank was unable to see his fiancée:

> *'She sat in the parlour with them herself; no one else would do as a chaperon [sic]. Of course, there would be no question of his going to Aunt Ellen's own sitting-room; nor obviously of her going to see him. One sometimes wonders how anyone was ever able to get engaged at all.'*

For the working and lower middle-classes, courtship is less restricted and while some attempt might be made to ensure that a young couple did not go out alone, this is not insisted upon. Sex before marriage is often common in country districts and among the lower working classes. Nevertheless, promiscuity was by no means rife; pre-marital sex was usually practised by couples

127

who were engaged to be married, and many Victorian brides were pregnant at the time of their nuptials.

For many working-class women, retaining their virtue and reputation was very important to increase the chances of a good marriage. Mrs Layton, born in Bethnal Green in 1855, worked in domestic service and her story is told in Margaret Llewelyn Davies' *Life As We Have Known It*. After a two-year engagement, Mrs Layton recalled:

> *'The man that I had promised to entrust my future life to made improper suggestions to me, and when I refused tried to overcome me by force. I am thankful I succeeded in defeating him. From that moment I lost all respect for him and, in spite of all his protestations of regret and promises that it should not occur again, I told him I would never forgive him, and broke off the engagement there and then.'*

From the mid-nineteenth century until the end of Queen Victoria's reign, the average age at marriage was 26 for women and 27-28 for men. If a man was apprenticed to a trade, he was expected to complete his apprenticeship before getting married and this could take up to seven years. It was also important to save enough money to set up a home in terms of furniture and furnishings before marriage, as well as to have the potential to be able to provide for any future children.

Mrs Layton became engaged again when she met her future husband at a mission hall. She recalled:

> *'I was engaged for three years before we were in a position to settle down, and then when everything was*

fixed up, rooms taken, furniture bought, arrangements made for the wedding to take place, the piano-making firm my husband worked for went bankrupt and he was thrown out of work. We decided not to put off the wedding, hoping he would soon find other work and we were married on December 2nd, 1882, he being twenty-seven and I twenty-six years of age.'

For many couples, courtship could be an even longer drawn-out affair. In 1887, Molly Hughes became engaged to her future husband Arthur on her twenty-first birthday. To her mother, Arthur 'seemed all that one could desire for a son-in-law, and he always remained as dear to her as one of her own sons'. Molly and Arthur struggled to find opportunities to see one another but this merely amused her mother. She said: 'Those little obstacles merely enhance the pleasure of your meeting. One kiss behind the door is worth ten in front of it'. It was to be ten years before the couple could marry, after Arthur had set up a fair practice at the Bar as a barrister and Molly had saved a nest egg of £200 from her work as a teacher.

In families where propriety was sacrosanct or the old values were adhered to, the suitor asked his beloved's father for her hand in marriage before an engagement was announced. If the father refused to give his consent, perhaps because the man was not wealthy enough, the couple could not marry unless they were of age (21). Some chose to ignore the disapproval of their parents and eloped to get married. The sexual age of consent was just 12 until 1875, so there was a distinct discrepancy between this and the marriageable age.

Engaged couples could take a few more liberties

than their unattached counterparts. They could go for walks together alone, hold hands in public and take an unchaperoned carriage ride, as long as it was not in an enclosed vehicle. Landowner Dearman Birchall was 45 when he married his second wife, Emily, who was just 20 years old. After he had proposed and they were officially engaged, Emily wrote to her intimate friend:

> *'Dearman came to dinner…He did not kiss me when he arrived, only shook hands very warmly. After dinner he and I were alone in the library for an hour till 9 o'clock when we went in for tea. He was very nice but didn't spoon or say anything special then…After prayers we had another tête à tête of ¾ hour which was delicious. He kissed me ever so many times and generally spooned a good deal and said "Oh my darling I do love you so", and was altogether most sweet and tender. He kissed me before parents on saying good-night, and again this morning. He has kissed me four times this morning though he went off at 10 o'clock to Leeds.'*

'Spooning' was simply Victorian slang for making romantic declarations of love. According to David Verey, the editor of their diaries and letters, the couple married in January 1873 and their European honeymoon tour lasted from January to June.

Tying the Knot

The wedding day itself also differed between the social classes. Albert Goodwin's working-class parents met at

130

the chapel they attended, where they also sang in the choir. His father was a china presser in a sanitary ware factory, and was later promoted to sanitary presser which paid more money. Albert's parents married in 1887; he tells the story in John Burnett's *Destiny Obscure*:

> 'No guests were expected as none had been invited. No best man, no bridesmaids because as they were to be married at Caverswell Church they had to walk 3 miles each way. Yes walk! Sunday morning 7.30 saw the start as they had to be at the Church for 9 am. When they got to the Church witnesses had to be found and my Father prevailed upon the Verger to be one. Mother went round the village, [and] got a woman as the other witness...Eventually the wedding took place... [The] wedding breakfast...consisted of 3 pairs of kippers which my Mother's Aunt had procured cheaply on the Saturday just before they closed.'

By contrast, no expense was spared for weddings within the gentry. Laura Green-Price's father was the squire of Norton Manor, about 20 miles from Shrewsbury. She recalls her marriage to Henry Hill Meredith in 1881 in *Destiny Obscure*:

> 'We had a large party in the house, twenty-two to dinner the night before, and sixty at Breakfast on the third...I had eight bridesmaids. Harry had three college friends who were very much liked, and very jolly...I had a hundred and forty presents, and among them a pearl necklet, pendant and earrings presented by the...people and tenants on the Norton Manor Estate. I wore them on my wedding day

which pleased the people. My wedding dress was cream satin and cream fur, and considered very pretty.'

When a woman married, until 1870, all her money and property legally passed to her husband. In that year, new legislation was introduced allowing married women to retain £200 of their own earnings. Twelve years later, the 1882 Married Women's Property Act allowed wives to own their own property inherited from relatives. Wishing to retain a degree of independence was the reason some working-class or lower middle-class women chose careers in nursing or in domestic service, perhaps as a cook or housekeeper, in preference to marriage.

For upper-class and upper middle-class women, it was far more difficult to deviate from the expected path of becoming a dutiful wife and mother. Florence Nightingale was born into a wealthy family but she wanted to do something useful. She wrote of the endless boredom of her domestic and social life before she went into nursing:

'O weary days! O evenings that never seem to end! For how many long years have I watched that drawing-room clock and thought it would never reach the ten.'

Unhappy unions

In law, Victorian women in troubled marriages had few options to leave them. Before 1857, divorce was beyond the reach of most people as it could only be obtained by an individual Act of Parliament – an extremely expensive process. Progress was achieved for men with the Matrimonial Causes Act of 1857, which allowed husbands to divorce their wives on grounds of adultery. Conversely, a woman could only divorce her husband if she was able to prove either cruelty, desertion, incest, rape, sodomy or bestiality, as well as adultery.

Even if a wife could obtain a divorce, her husband could legally restrict access to their children if they were over the age of seven. One other way of escaping the relationship legally was through obtaining an annulment based on non-consummation of the marriage, a route Effie Gray took to nullify her five-year union with John Ruskin in 1854, marrying the artist John Millais the following year.

High-profile divorce cases examined the alleged misdemeanours of husbands and wives, and also identified the other 'involved parties'. Newspapers went into great detail to report on the salacious gossip and scandal that went with each trial, and the public eagerly lapped it up, buying copies in their thousands. One such case was begun in 1869 when Charles Mordaunt, a Conservative MP and baronet, filed for divorce from his wife Harriet, who was accused of adultery with numerous men. It was rumoured that one of the men she had an affair with was none other than the then Prince of Wales, Edward VII, but this was never proved. After a seven-day trial, Lady Mordaunt was deemed to be suffering from 'puerperal mania' and spent the rest of her life in a lunatic asylum.

Other divorce trials were more straightforward when they were uncontested, such as that experienced by H. G. Wells, who separated from his wife Isabel in

1894 after he fell in love with one of his students, Amy Catherine Robbins (known as Jane). As he explained to his father in a letter dated that year,

'The matter is extremely simple. Last January I ran away with a young lady student of mine to London. It's not a bit of good dilating on that matter because the mischief is done and what remains now is to get affairs straight again. Isabel left the house at Sutton and went to Hampstead where she is now living (at my expense) and she has now got through about half the necessary divorce proceedings against me. I expect to be divorced early next year and then I shall marry Miss Robbins. The house at Sutton the landlord took off my hands upon my paying the rent up to June. Since then I have been in apartments with Miss Robbins (passing as my wife).'

H. G. Wells married Jane Robbins in 1895 and their marriage lasted until her death; with Jane's consent, Wells had numerous affairs (and children) with other women.

Tight-knit families could be protective of daughters or sisters, even after they married. William Andrews was the manager of a ribbon factory in Coventry. His sister Ann married George Carter, a farmer, in March 1862 and had a daughter nine months later. On 16 March 1863, William wrote in his diary:

'Receive a telegram today at 1.30 from High Cross, that Carter is going to sell all and is beating Ann. Take a van and go over with father. Find Carter mad drunk and Ann at neighbour Scotten's. We visit a magistrate and decide that Ann shall take a warrant against him for assault.'

The next day, Ann obtained a warrant and later that night, her husband's father drove him to Rugby station, intending for him to leave forever, and he was not seen after this. By 23 March, Ann had taken forcible possession of the house at High Cross and arranged for a sale to take place. Three days later, George Carter reappeared there but luckily Ann was at home in Coventry. A week later, the sale at High Cross went through and George Carter was bailed to appear in court.

On 1 April, William records in his diary: 'G. C. knocks at our house at 12h. 15m. this morning, and demands his wife. Father threatens to give him in charge, on which he goes off. G. C. hanging round the neighbourhood this morning and annoying the family. He is given in charge, but let off by the superintendent on promising not to repeat it'. The day after, William wrote: 'Father, Ann and Mr Davis go over to Lutterworth. The case is compromised. A deed of separation is drawn up. G.C. is to allow 2/6 per week for the child, and his father becomes responsible for the payment of the £20 money lent'.

Without the support of her family or the finances to meet legal costs, Ann could not have brought about this legal separation. It was not the end of the matter, as on 1 May, George Carter sent an advertisement to the *Coventry Standard* that he would not be responsible for his wife's debts. At the Andrews family's suggestion, the newspaper returned the advertisement to George Carter. Ann went to keep house for her brother William, she 'being without occupation'.

William's diary mentions his brother-in-law again on 11 November 1864: 'George Carter leaves High Cross about this date with his woman, said to be gone to Canada'. Starting a new life overseas was an easy way for George Carter to distance himself from the mess of his marriage to Ann. She did not, however, have that option. Most working-class couples did not have the means to bring about a legal separation. 'Living in sin' with their next partner or becoming their 'common law' wife or husband was the only choice. Although illegal, bigamy was also resorted to by some people who were anxious to forget their old lives and start again with a new spouse.

STARTING A FAMILY

For some working-class families, it was traditional to have large numbers of children to make up for the high proportion that would not survive to adulthood; at least one or two offspring was considered necessary if their parents were to avoid the workhouse in old age. Aside from this, large families of six, seven or eight children among the working classes were usually a result of ignorance about contraception. It was commonly known that breastfeeding could help reduce the chances of conceiving because it delayed ovulation, but this only worked up to around six months after birth, and only if feeding was done very frequently throughout the day. Other than this and the very unreliable withdrawal method, the working classes had little knowledge of birth control. It was, however, more widely used by the middle classes from the 1860s onwards. There was also disagreement among medical men about exactly when in a woman's cycle the 'safe period' should be.

In *The Elements of Social Science* (1854), Dr George Drysdale examined whether sexual intercourse using contraception could be practised 'without causing moral and physical harm'. He concluded that withdrawal is 'physically injurious, and is apt to produce nervous disorder and sexual enfeeblement and congestion', while the sheath 'dulls the enjoyment, and frequently produces impotence in the man and disgust in both parties'. Drysdale was adamant that any preventive means 'must be used by the *woman*, as it spoils the passion and impulsiveness of the venereal act, if the man has to think of them'.

Knowledge about contraception did not reach the working classes who needed it most, nor were the methods affordable to them. The campaigners Annie Besant and Charles Bradlaugh wanted to change this. They published a booklet called *The Fruits of Philosophy* in 1877, explaining how to use pessaries, sponges, condoms and vaginal douches. For their efforts, they were both convicted of publishing 'an obscene libel' but their prison sentence was quashed on appeal. Soon after, in the 1880s and 1890s, contraceptives become more widely available and you will see them advertised by travelling lecturers, in chemists' shops and in public conveniences. The mass production of condoms, now made of rubber, makes them more affordable, and they can be bought for as little as ½d each by the second half of the nineteenth century. The cost still makes them prohibitive for the lower working classes.

Whether unmarried and in domestic service, or married with too many mouths to feed already, many desperate women tried to end unwanted pregnancies by bringing about a miscarriage or, more rarely, obtaining an abortion.

Home remedies for abortions include drinking numerous pints of gin, inserting knitting needles into the vagina, and deliberately falling downstairs. Diachylon, a plaster made from lead, is commonly used as an ointment for cuts and sores but it was also known to cause an abortion if ingested as a tablet. Another option was 'hickery-pickery', a compound of aloes and canella bark.

Newspapers regularly advertised pills for 'menstrual irregularities', which, in fact, had abortifacient properties. In 1898, a sensational blackmail case revealed that the Chrimes brothers from London had extorted money from female customers who had bought their (supposed) abortifacient pills. They sent letters which threatened to tell the authorities that the women had committed an act punishable by penal servitude, unless they paid £2 2s (two guineas). Twelve thousand women were contacted, indicating how widespread the practice was, and within three or four days, £800 had been paid to them.

Obtaining an abortion from a herbalist, doctor or midwife was hugely risky for both the pregnant woman and the person carrying out the procedure. Procuring an abortion by using an instrument or chemical substances was illegal, and anyone prosecuted could be sentenced to penal servitude. Cases of procuring an abortion often came to light if a woman died as a result. In December 1895, Sarah Ann Eden, a midwife from Warwickshire, was convicted of the murder of Rebecca Simister, a mother of six children who could not face a seventh confinement. Rebecca died after begging the midwife to bring about a miscarriage. The post-mortem revealed the cause of death was blood poisoning 'arising from punctures by an instrument'. Sarah Ann was convicted of murder and the death sentence was passed upon her, although this was later commuted to penal servitude for life.

THE OLDEST PROFESSION

Walk the streets of any large city in England and you will not fail to notice the large number of prostitutes. In fact, if you're male, do not be surprised if you are propositioned on a daily basis, especially in the parks and pleasure gardens. Hippolyte Taine recalled London, particularly Haymarket and the Strand in the evening:

> 'you cannot walk a hundred yards without knocking into twenty streetwalkers: some of them ask you for a glass of gin; other says, "It's for my rent, mister." The impression is not one of debauchery but of abject, miserable poverty. One is sickened and wounded by this deplorable procession in those monumental streets. It seemed as if I were watching a march past of dead women. Here is a festering sore, the real sore on the body of English society.'

Many girls in cities like London became prostitutes after being tricked into giving up their virginity by women whose sole objective was to obtain virgins for their rich male clients. In 1885, when W. T. Stead interviewed two London procuresses for *Pall Mall Gazette*, he asked where the girls came from: 'Nurse-girls and shop-girls…and sometimes cooks and other servants…Young girls from the country, fresh and rosy, are soon picked up in the shops or as they run errands.

But nurse-girls are the great field'. They added:

> *'Every morning at this time of the year my friend and I are up at seven, and after breakfast we put a shawl round our shoulders and off we go to scour the park. Hyde Park and the Green Park are the best in the morning; Regent's Park in the afternoon. As we go coasting along, we keep a sharp look out for any likely girl, and having spotted one, we make up to her; and week after week we see her as often as possible, until we are sufficiently in her confidence to suggest how easy it is to earn a few pounds by meeting a man...*
>
> *'Thus we have always a crop of maids ripening, and at any time we can undertake to deliver a maid if we get due notice...Sometimes we have no end of trouble with the little fools. You see they often have no idea in the world as to what being seduced is. We do not take the trouble to explain, and it is enough for us if the girl willingly consents to see or to meet or to have a game with a rich gentleman.'*

Shocking though this is (and the Victorian middle classes were appalled by Stead's articles), very little was done about it. When Stead asked the former director of the Criminal Investigation Department at New Scotland Yard for his opinion about the forced seductions, he commented: 'It will go on, and you cannot help it, as long as men have money, procuresses are skilful, and women are weak and inexperienced'. Stead tried to do something about the problem himself by publicising how easy it was to procure a young girl for immoral purposes. He arranged to 'purchase' Eliza Armstrong for £5, and once the transaction was complete, she was given over into the care of the Salvation Army. Nevertheless, this stunt landed him in court with abduction charges, and he was jailed for three months. The legal age of sexual consent was, however, raised to 16 later that year.

First-time visitors to Victorian England would do well to heed the advice of Max O'Rell in *John Bull and His Island* (1884):

'*A woman alone is safer in the streets of London than an unprotected male. A woman risks having her purse stolen; a man risks more: he risks his reputation. He may be stopped by a woman who will say to him in an indignant tone: "Give me five shillings, or I will call a policeman. You have insulted me!" Or, it may be, a young girl, often a little girl, who will come up to you and politely ask you to tell her the time. Without suspecting harm, you take out your watch and you are immediately surrounded by several individuals who rob you, or accuse you of having insulted the girl.*

'*Dreading a scandal, you pay rather than be dragged into an unpleasant affair...I know few men in London to whom this kind of adventure has not happened once at least. The parks and the Thames Embankment especially are places that every man who values his honour should carefully avoid, even in broad daylight...At night-fall, the parks and unfrequented places are entirely given up to thieves and prostitutes.*'

For some girls, like out-of-work servants, hop-pickers and flower-girls, prostitution is often a seasonal form of employment, especially in cities like London. In a diary entry for 17 August 1860, Arthur Munby wrote:

'In Oxford Street a fashionable prostitute accosted me who once before had begged me to go home with her; & she now explained her importunity by saying "All my gentlemen have left town, and I really am so hard up – I shall have to give up my lodgings!" "Then why not go out of town too?" "I've nowhere to go to!" This, spoken by a girl who though not interesting was elegant & well-dressed, gives one a sad sense of the loneliness of such a life – and a glimpse also of the embarrassment which besets these London butterflies when the season is over. She was a farmer's daughter from near Chesterfield; & came to town, nominally to be a draper's assistant, but really to become of her own accord what she is. N.B. After nine months, her family still think she is at the shop.'

Hardened prostitutes and newcomers alike were subject to the cruel legislation known as the Contagious Diseases Acts, passed between 1864 and 1869. These laws were enforced in garrison towns and ports, designed to protect their male clients, and they embody the Victorian double standard. Any woman suspected of prostitution could be arrested, forcibly examined for venereal disease and hospitalised if necessary. Men who used prostitutes were not subject to any such checks, and if they were married, they brought venereal diseases such as syphilis into the home, and infected their unsuspecting wives.

Josephine Butler led the campaign to bring about a repeal of the Acts, forming the Ladies' National Association to attack the classification of these women as 'pure' or 'impure'. Through her influence, other respectable women began to support prostitutes driven to the profession through poverty or no fault of their own.

With a greater knowledge of Victorian courtship under your belt, you may be able to guess the status of couples' relationships when you see them at the theatre, pleasure garden or seaside – all ideal places to begin a flirtation.

Chapter Nine
Amusements and Entertainments

'At Shanklin one has to adopt the detestable custom of bathing in drawers. If ladies don't like to see men naked why don't they keep away from the sight? To-day I had a pair of drawers given me which I could not keep on. The rough waves stripped them off and tore them down round my ankles. While thus fettered I was seized and flung down by a heavy sea which retreating suddenly left me lying naked on the sharp shingle from which I rose streaming with blood. After this I took the wretched and dangerous rag off and of course there were some ladies looking on as I came up out of the water.'
(Reverend Francis Kilvert's diary, 12 June 1874)

During your visit to Victorian England, you'll come across many tourists who are discovering more about the country in which they live. The advent of rail travel opens up a whole new world for people from all walks of life, particularly the curious middle and industrious working classes, and they come in enthusiastic droves to take an excursion to the seaside, see the Great Exhibition, visit the countryside or enjoy a trip to the capital for the first time.

It's a new age of leisure, especially after the Bank Holidays Act of 1871, which designates Easter Monday, Whit Monday, the first Monday in August and Boxing Day as public holidays. Half-day working on Saturdays becomes more common from the 1870s, leaving Sunday as the day of the week when the working man can take a true holiday. Unpaid holidays were already common, for instance, in Lancashire and Cheshire during Wakes Weeks, and at festival times throughout the year, but holidays with pay do not exist until late in the Victorian period. Workers for the Great Northern Railway were the first to get regular paid holidays in 1872, according to Pamela Horn in *Pleasures and Pastimes in Victorian Britain*. The Amalgamated Society of Railway Servants successfully negotiated one week's paid holiday after five years' service in 1897. Other industries followed suit as and when the workers' unions reached agreement with the employers.

THE GREAT EXHIBITION

If you visit in 1851, then a trip to the Great Exhibition at the Crystal Palace in Hyde Park is an absolute must. Its full title is 'The Great Exhibition of the Works of Industry of all Nations of 1851' and there are 13,937 exhibitors. You'll need to allow plenty of time to look around as there are 100,000 exhibits. When the exhibition closes in October 1851, more than six million people have seen it. The organisers make sure there are tickets to suit all pockets with three-guinea season tickets for men and two guineas for women, as well as days when admission costs as little as one shilling.

On 'shilling days', the class of visitor is very different from those on more expensive entrance days. Henry Mayhew describes the first 'Shilling Day' at the Great

Exhibition: 'The ladies are all 'got up' in their brightest-coloured bonnets and polkas…while the gentlemen in green or brown felt 'wide-awakes', or fluffy beaver hats, and with the cuffs of their best coats, and the bottoms of their best trousers turned up, are marching heavily on – some with babies in their arms, others with baskets, and others carrying corpulent cotton umbrellas'.

Inside, the scene is very different from the first week or two:

> *'Those who are now to be found there, have come to look at the Exhibition, and not to make an exhibition of themselves. There is no air of display about them – no social falsity…The jewels and the tapestry, and the Lyons silks are now the sole objects of attraction. The shilling folk may be an 'inferior' class of visitors, but at least, they know something about the works of industry, and what they do not know, they have come to learn… Around the fountain are gathered families, drinking out of small mugs, inscribed as 'presents for Charles or Mary'; while all over the floor, walk where you will – are strewn the greasy papers of devoured sandwiches.'*

After the exhibition closes, the Crystal Palace is rebuilt in a different and enlarged form on Penge Common near Sydenham. After a visit in 1855, Nathaniel Hawthorne described the Crystal Palace as 'a gigantic toy for the English people to play with. The design seems to be to reproduce all past ages, by representing the features of their interior architecture, costume, religion, domestic life and everything that can be expressed by paint and plaster; and, likewise, to bring all climates and regions of the earth within these enchanted precincts, with their inhabitants and animals in living semblance, and their vegetable productions, as far as possible, alive and real...The Indian, the Egyptian, and especially the Arabian, courts are admirably executed. I never saw or conceived anything so gorgeous as the Alhambra'.

FROM BEARDED LADIES TO BALLOON-HEADED BABIES

Travelling circuses bring a different kind of entertainment to people living in out of the way places who had little opportunity for visiting large towns. While on holiday at Windermere in 1895, Beatrix Potter 'went to see Ginnet's Circus at Ambleside and had a good laugh'. She wrote in her journal: 'I would go any distance to see a Caravan (barring lion-taming), it is the only species of entertainment I care for'. In her opinion:

'The most skilful performers were two men on parallel bars, and Herr Wartenburg the Barrel-King, who climbed on to a high seat and, having wiped it with a pocket handkerchief, laid himself on his velveteen back with his heels in the air, and danced wrong side up to the tune of The Keelrow against a cylinder, and then an immense barrel, I suppose inflated with gas. He danced his feet most gracefully, in little pointed shoes. The performing-dogs turned back-somersaults with agility, and one small poodle dressed in clown's jacket and trousers skipped energetically on its hind legs, two persons turning the rope.'

147

'Lord' George Sanger's Family Circus was one of the best known and he toured the provincial and metropolitan fairs in the spring and summer, wintering near London. Wombwell's was the most famous of the travelling menageries; it styled itself 'the wandering teachers of Natural History' and had more than 600 animals, birds and reptiles on display.

With their penchant for spectacles of all kinds, you'll discover that the Victorians love to gawp at 'freak shows', which exhibit humans or animals who do not have 'normal' bodies. These shows travel the country, while some have permanent exhibitions in London. All have over-the-top advertisements which publicise their living curiosities, often with wild inaccuracy. They include extraordinarily fat or thin people, 'giants' and 'midgets', conjoined twins and people from far flung corners of the globe. Bear in mind that the 'giant Amazon queen' may not actually be nine feet tall and that the 'living mermaid' may, in fact, be a trick. Tom Norman, the 'Silver King', was a travelling showman who exhibited human and animal curiosities. His acts included Eliza Jenkins, the 'Skeleton Woman'; the 'Balloon-Headed Baby', and 'the woman who bit live rat heads off'. In his autobiography, he claimed: 'You could exhibit anything in those days. Yes, anything from a needle to an anchor, a flea to an elephant, a bloater you could exhibit as a whale. It was not the show, it was the tale that you told'.

MUSIC AND MELODRAMA

You'll find that going to the music hall or theatre is

an extremely popular way to spend an evening in Victorian England. Music halls originate from the singing saloons attached to public houses, as well as the entertainments put on in pleasure gardens, saloon theatres and 'penny gaffs' (cheap theatres).

Two of the first prototypes were the Star at Bolton, opened in 1832, and the Canterbury which was opened in Lambeth by Charles Morton in the 1840s. The entertainment included 'glees, madrigals, choruses, songs and comic renditions under the direction of a chairman-compère', according to Pamela Horn. Mondays and Saturdays are the most popular evenings when 'hundreds of people would wait at the doors for it to open, so that the street outside would be almost blocked'. In a bid to encourage women to the music hall, 'Ladies' Thursdays' were introduced, when women could attend if accompanied by a gentleman. Morton was keen to promote a respectable reputation and his premises also offered a library, reading-room and picture gallery. In 1861, he opened London's first purpose-built music hall, the Oxford. This had fixed seating facing the stage, unlike the earlier halls with tables and chairs where visitors could eat, drink and smoke.

Music halls were especially popular with the working and lower middle-classes, and by the early 1890s, about 300 were open across Britain. You have plenty of alternatives too, with assembly rooms and parish halls licensed for music and dancing.

The most successful music hall performers became household names. Dan Leno was especially well-known for playing the dame in Christmas pantomimes and Vesta Tilley was famous for her male impersonator act. Another music hall star was Marie Lloyd, who clearly knew what her audiences wanted. Pamela Horn quotes her as saying, "You take the pit on a Saturday night or a Bank Holiday. You don't suppose they want Sunday school stuff do you? They want lively stuff with music they can learn quickly. Why, if I was to try and sing highly moral songs they would fire ginger beer bottles and beer mugs at me. They don't pay their sixpences at a Music Hall to hear the Salvation Army".

Food and soft drinks could be bought at the music hall by those who did not want alcohol. Joseph Stamper regularly went with his father to The People's Palace music hall in St Helen's in the 1890s. In *So Long Ago*, he recalls: 'Eccles cakes full of currants were one penny or a halfpenny according to size; pop was one penny a bottle; and oranges were three a penny...Many a time...when I smell an orange, I am back in the People's Palace, a small boy seated next to father, sucking an orange while he sipped his bottle of pop'.

Unlike music halls, after the mid-nineteenth century, you'll find that theatre audiences are made up of all social classes. Admittedly, there are separate entrances and exits, and defined areas for each class so that they do not intermingle. The boxes are for the wealthy upper classes, the middle classes sit in the pit, while the gallery is reserved for the working classes. According to *Cornish's Guide to Birmingham* for 1858, the theatre in New Street has a 'commodious pit, two rows of boxes and an extensive gallery' and can accommodate 2,000 people. The entrance to the boxes is in New Street; to the pit, through a small passage in Lower Temple Street; and to the gallery from a small street at the back of the theatre. The cost of admission is three shillings for a dress box, two shillings for an upper box, one shilling for the pit and sixpence for the gallery.

'In order to get a place from which you can witness the performance while seated, it is necessary to be at the entrance at least half an hour before the doors open', advises Thomas Wright in *Some Habits and Customs of the Working Classes* (1867). 'And when they do open you have to take part in a rush and struggle the fierceness of which can only be credited by those who have taken part in such encounters'. Wright also vividly describes the type of people who sit in the gallery, dividing them into 'the roughs, the hypocrites or snobs and the orderlies'. The roughs are the most numerous, consisting of:

'those who come to the theatre with unwashed faces and in ragged and dirty attire, who bring bottles of drink with them, who will smoke despite of the notice that 'smoking is strictly prohibited' and that 'officers will be in attendance'; who favour the band with a stamping accompaniment, and take the most noisy part in applauding or giving 'the call' to the performers. The females of this class are generally accompanied by infants, who are sure to cry and make a disturbance at some interesting point in the performance.

'The snobs comprise those who will tell you that they prefer the gallery to any other part of the house, and that they would still go into it if the price of admission...was as high as that charged...to the pit or boxes; nevertheless, they seem very ill at ease in the place of their choice, and shrink from the glances of the occupants of the pit and

*boxes...The orderlies are those who, while they admit
that the gallery is the least comfortable, and it may be the
least respectable part of the house, and that they would
much rather be in the boxes, go into the gallery because
it is the cheapest part of the house – because they can go
into that part twice for the same amount of money that
they would have to pay to go into any other part once.'*

A final warning: the people who sit in the galleries also
have a tendency to discharge 'nutshells, peas, orange-
peel, and other annoying, though harmless missiles' at
the heads of the occupants below.

PARKS AND PLEASURE GARDENS

Parks were another source of pleasure for the
Victorians. Although London already had Hyde Park,
Green Park and Regent's Park, they are owned by the
Royal Family. Princes Park in Liverpool was the first
purpose-built public park, although it was financed
privately; it was designed by Joseph Paxton with a
lake and serpentine carriageway, and was opened in
1843. Four years later, Paxton used a similar design in
Birkenhead's municipal park, the first to be built with
public finances. Other large towns and cities followed
suit, recognising the need to provide open spaces for
the urban population.

In London, there are also pleasure gardens such
as Vauxhall and Cremorne. At Vauxhall Gardens,
Max Schlesinger saw 'music, singing, horsemanship,
illuminations, dancing, rope-dancing, acting, comic

songs, hermits, gypsies, and fireworks'. Once an exclusive attraction for the gentry, in Victorian times Vauxhall was open to all ranks and classes and was well past its heyday by the time it finally closed in 1859. The most famous London pleasure gardens were those at Cremorne in King's Road, Chelsea. Christopher Hibbert describes 'the theatres and side-shows, shooting galleries, fortune-tellers and tightrope-walkers, circuses, water pageants and medieval tournaments' on offer to visitors.

Unfortunately, there were also 'numerous pickpockets and whores, rowdy boys and drunks', leading to an unwholesome reputation and Cremorne's eventual closure in 1877. The Crystal Palace Company's pleasure gardens at Sydenham were much more respectable, offering 'musical concerts, exhibitions of painting and sculpture, tropical trees, architectural models and full-scale bronze dinosaurs'.

BY THE SEASIDE

Numerous seaside resorts develop in the Victorian period in parallel with the railway network. They include Ramsgate, Broadstairs, Margate, Blackpool, Bournemouth, Southport and Weston-super-Mare, as well as Ventnor and Ryde on the Isle of Wight. 'Not all were fashionable, but all provided sea air, damp lodgings, bad food, and two lots of bathing machines separated by a good stretch of shore: one for women bathers, the other for men', comments Elizabeth Burton.

You'll quickly discover that each resort is aimed

at a particular social class. In the south of England, Christopher Hibbert comments that 'the genteel and retiring [went] to Lyme Regis, Broadstairs and Folkestone; the fashionable to Eastbourne, Bognor and Cowes [and] the less well-to-do went to Margate, Ramsgate or Southend'. There, the visitors 'walked along the pier which no self-respecting resort could do without, or congregated at the water's edge, peering out to sea through telescopes, knitting in the shade of umbrellas and parasols, reading newspapers and resisting the importunities of men selling ships in bottles and saucers of whelks; their children, as Frith depicted them on Ramsgate sands, running with bucket and spade between the Punch and Judy show and the nigger minstrels'.

In the north, although the railway arrives in Blackpool in 1846, it is not until the 1860s that the town significantly developed as a tourist resort. This was 'about the same time that Lancashire's workforce became entitled to statutory holidays', as John Hannavy points out in *The English Seaside in Victorian and Edwardian Times*. By the end of the Victorian period, the resort is equipped with three piers and receives about three million visitors each year.

Piers with great pleasure pavilions were not introduced until the 1880s and 1890s, often replacing earlier structures. Great Yarmouth's original Britannia Pier offered a wide range of amusements for visitors including 'the Original Continental 6d Bazaar, brass-band concerts, an aquarium and even a photographic studio adjacent to the Refreshment Room'.

One of the best childhood treats at the end of the

nineteenth century was 'a train trip to Brighton, 2/6 return for the day'. A London contributor to Pat Barr's *I Remember* recalls that 'the carriages were long and divided into four or five compartments with partitions which did not reach to the top. One could see into the next compartment or even climb into it. The seats were wooden benches. These trips were gay affairs, buskers would board the train at various stops and give the passengers a sing-song till the next stop, then the hat would be passed round and over the partitions'.

Sea bathing was a major attraction of this outing. The contributor continues:

'We would make for the sea, hire a bathing suit and towel, and disrobe in the big bathing huts on wheels. Then a horse was hitched on and the machine taken to the water's edge. Ladies were firmly secured to the machine by a rope for safety. There was no mixed bathing and gentlemen bathed further along the beach. When we came out of the sea, we gave our suits and towels to an old woman who sat at a wooden tub and ringer attached, she would wash them and hang them on a line to dry. There were two concert parties, several buskers and a Punch and Judy show on the sands.'

If you're visiting the seaside, you'll find that it is the custom for men to bathe naked, but women wear 'either a voluminous, sleeved bathing dress tied at the ankles by string, or a heavy all-enveloping, tent-like cloak'. Women did no proper swimming, as they were simply dipped by the bathing-machine attendant. Queen Victoria had a rather more luxurious bathing-machine at Osborne House, her home on the Isle of Wight. She undressed in it and bathed in the sea for the first time in 1847, writing in her journal: 'I thought it delightful till I put my head under water, when I thought I should be stifled'. If you use a bathing machine, remember to tip the attendant.

A SPORTING NATION

The English have always enjoyed playing sports and ancient games like football and cricket become more organised in the nineteenth century. The Football Association is founded in 1863 and 'soccer' clubs spring up around the country. At first, many of them have public school or upper-class origins, but the working classes soon adopt the games for themselves. By the 1880s, all the main features of the modern game are in place: the 'leagues of teams visiting each other's grounds; charges for admission; 'professionals…and in the wake of the fans, roughs and vandals', according to Geoffrey Best. In the industrial districts of the north, large crowds pay to watch the leading clubs of the day.

The game of cricket just before Queen Victoria came to the throne is described by Mary Russell Mitford in *Our Village* as 'a real solid old-fashioned match between neighbouring parishes, where each attacks the other for honour and a supper, glory and half-a-crown a man'. Cricket develops as a sport earlier than football, helped by the railway network. There are local clubs and county teams, made up of both professionals and amateurs like the supremely talented W. G. Grace. The first professional

England touring side goes to North America in 1859, followed by Australia in 1861 and South Africa in 1888. The Australian team visits England in 1878 and by 1900, the biennial Test Match tours between the two countries are in place. New games like lawn tennis also become popular during this period, as well as golf which had long been played in Scotland.

One sporting occasion unites all the social classes: the Epsom Derby, which was both a race week and a fair. In this week, all roads to Epsom were 'blocked with every conceivable type of vehicle and mode of conveyance; farm carts, gipsy wagons, ancient coaches, smart new equipages, push barrows, men on horseback, wagons and pedestrians,' writes Elizabeth Burton. Nearby, 'fairground people always set up their attractions… while vendors of food and drink with their trays slung about their necks catered for the mass appetite'.

Hippolyte Taine vividly describes Derby Day in the 1870s:

'There are gypsies everywhere, singers and dancers grotesquely got up as negroes; booths for shooting with bow and carbine, cheap-jacks selling watch-chains with a torrent of eloquence, games of skittles, and Aunt Sally, all kinds of musicians, and the most astonishing procession of cabs, coaches, droskis [sic], four-in-hands, each with its basket of pies and pastries, cold meats, melons, fruit and wine, especially champagne. They are being unpacked; everyone is going to eat and drink, it will restore and raise their animal spirits; noisy, full-blooded enjoyment and loud, candid laughter are products of a full stomach…
…the appearance of the numerous poor is a painful

sight: they try to sell you a ha'penny doll, souvenirs of the Derby, persuade you to try your luck at the Aunt Sally shies, or to have your boots shined. Almost all of them look like wretched, beaten, mangy curs, waiting to be thrown a bone without much hope. They have walked here during the night and count for their dinner on the crumbs from the vast al fresco banquet.'

LADIES (AND GENTLEMEN) OF LEISURE

For the wealthy upper classes, the London 'season' was the highlight of their calendar. This period of social activities began after Easter in April or May and ended in August before the grouse-shooting season began on the 'Glorious Twelfth'. Those who usually lived at their country residences would decamp to the capital to their town quarters or to a rented house; attendance was particularly important if a daughter was due to 'come out' and be presented at court as a debutante. The London 'season' involved a hectic succession of balls, dinner parties, banquets, opera and theatre visits, as well as garden parties and sporting events like the Henley Regatta, Ascot and the Derby.

Frances Greville (later Countess of Warwick) described the daily ride in Hyde Park during the 'season', as quoted by J. F. C. Harrison:

'Here the small circle of Society with the big 'S' was sure of meeting all its members on morning ride or drive, or in the late afternoon between tea and dinner, in what was practically a daily Society Garden Party!

[We] chatted of the social round – of future meetings, of dances, lunches and dinners within 'the Circle'. My horses were so well known that they always made a stir. One 'booked' friends for luncheon, and perhaps drove them down Piccadilly prancing on the wide sweep of pavement, glancing up at the Turf Club window as a possible place to find an extra man for a dinner-party'.

When money was no object, the development of the railways meant infinite opportunities for continental travel and further afield. Dearman Birchall was a country squire with an estate in Gloucestershire. He and his wife Emily frequently holidayed in Europe, leaving their young children at home. In late January 1880, they embarked on a tour of Spain. At the time, Emily was six months pregnant. Dearman wrote in his diary:

'We left by Calais boat with a smooth sea. We arrived in Paris at 6.10 and left Catarozzi to pass the luggage and drove to the Orleans Station where we dined at the buffet getting away by the 7.15 pm train for Toulouse. We had a luxurious 1st class carriage. The hot-water tins were long enough for two of them to go the whole width of the carriage. They were changed every hour and a half all night. Two lamps with silk shades. The trimmings of the carriage all in beautiful order. The line is very smooth and we slept well. The appointments shame our English railways. It was a beautiful moonlit night but the frost was not intense.'

In early March, while the couple were staying in Gibraltar, Emily went into premature labour and gave birth to a daughter at the hotel. Not wanting to cut short their planned tour or to risk taking their three-week-old baby overland through Spain, they decided to send her home by sea on a P&O steamer. Emily wrote that the baby was to be accompanied by their courier and a 'most excellent, kind, nice, superior woman whom we have been most fortunate in securing'. The couple continued on their holiday, visiting Cadiz, Seville, Madrid and San Sebastian among other places. This was 'a round trip of 4,382 miles taking 240 hours' travelling time', according to David Verey, the editor of their diaries and letters. The trip was cut short on 13 April when they received news that Dearman's uncle had died – they were back in London two days later.

SAY 'CHEESE'

The invention and subsequent popularity of photography means that you can take home a souvenir from Victorian England. In the late 1850s, the number of photographic studios increases dramatically with the introduction of the glass positive. For the first time, photographs were affordable for working people. The cheap studios of the late 1850s and early 1860s are usually in an upper storey of a building to take advantage of the light, so it is necessary for photographers to employ a 'tout' to patrol the street and alert illiterate potential customers. Targeting the working classes, these photographers work on Sundays. From 1861, most photographs are in the popular *carte de visite* format (the size of a visiting card), unless you can afford the larger, more expensive cabinet portrait.

In *The Victorians: Photographic Portraits*, Audrey Linkman quotes from *The Photographic News* (1861) which derides the cheap studios:

> 'To every one...there is attached one or more hired bullies called 'door men', whose vocation it is to prowl up and down before the portal of the unwholesome temple of black art, to thrust villainous portraits into the faces of passers by; to make use of filthy and ribald talk to the giddy girls who stop to stare at the framed display of portraits; to exchange blackguard repartee with the 'door men' of some neighbouring and rival studio; and, if need be, to assist their employers in ejecting, pummelling, and otherwise maltreating troublesome customers.'

If you visit a photographic studio before the 1880s, you will find that posing stands and back-rests are necessary to keep you in position so that you don't move during the exposure time. This may only be for five or six seconds but any movement will blur the image. Contrary to popular belief, smiling is allowed, although men are expected to appear more serious than women or children.

In 1896, the new cinematograph process wows the Victorian public. Although there are not yet any cinemas, very short films of not more than a minute start to be shown in theatres and music halls. According to Leslie Baily, the first public film show in Britain 'to attract wide interest' is given by Monsieur Lumière at the London Polytechnic, repeated at the

Empire music-hall in Leicester Square. Lumière's 'French Cinématographe' is a result of improving Edison's Kinetoscope. A London scientific instrument-maker named Robert W. Paul also gets in on the act in the same year, inventing a film projector called a Theatregraph. He films the Derby and shows the film at the Alhambra music hall in Leicester Square. Ironically, this new technology led to the eventual demise of the music hall and ushered in a new type of entertainment which remains popular today.

Having explored the towns and cities at length, slow down the pace a little and take a trip to the countryside where you'll find evidence of many ancient and colourful customs and traditions!

Chapter Ten
Customs and Traditions

'I remained at Matlock through the day, and went over to a village called Bonsal, where they were holding a wake. Many of the principal villages have this kind of holiday, which begins commonly on Sunday, and lasts through the whole week. The villagers give themselves up to frolicking; the neighbourhood turns out; the tramps and vagabonds come from the country round; the gipsies have an encampment near; and in general the lowest class of people, for no others attend, devote themselves to play, and frolic, and drunkenness.'
(Henry Colman, *European Life and Manners*, 1850)

If you want to experience Victorian customs and traditions at first hand, head for the countryside. This is where ancient celebrations, like the wake week Henry Colman attended in Derbyshire, are zealously protected and upheld. There you will find the calendar packed with special feast days and holidays connected with the seasons. Those who migrate to the towns to find work lose this connection with the land and the farming year, which is one reason they are so enthusiastic about observing the four official Bank Holidays introduced after 1871.

163

HIGH DAYS AND HOLIDAYS

In small rural villages, the traditional festivals of the annual feast, May Day and the harvest home are celebrated year in, year out. J. Arthur Gibbs interviewed an elderly labourer for *A Cotswold Village* (1898), who remembered traditions of the past:

> *'Fifty years ago 'twere all mirth and jollity. There was four feasts in the year for us folk. First of all there was the savers' feast – that would be about the end of April; then came the sheep-shearer's feast – there'd be about fifteen of us would sit down after sheep-shearing, and we'd be singing best part of the night, and plenty to eat and drink; next came the feast for the reapers, when the corn was cut about August; and last of all, the harvest home in September.'*

Plough Monday is the first festival in the farming year and is the first day after Christmas that ploughing can resume. 'It was the ancient custom for farm labourers, tricked out in ribbons and scarves, to drag a plough around the parish calling at doors to ask for money to pay for festivities – drinking, sword-dancing and a mummers' play, which symbolised the end of the old year and the start of the new', comments David Souden in *The Victorian Village*.

May Day has been celebrated since ancient times, and you'll find that country villages cling to the tradition, crowning a May Queen and enjoying music, dancing and feasting. William Howitt describes the elaborate May Day festival in Huntingdonshire in *The*

Rural Life of England (1838):

> *'The children still exhibit garlands. They suspend a sort of crown of hoops, wreathed and ornamented with flowers, ribbons, handkerchiefs, necklaces, silver spoons, and whatever finery can be procured, at a considerable height above the road, by a rope extending from chimney to chimney of the cottages, while they attempt to throw their balls over it from side to side, singing, and begging halfpence' for a festive tea.*

The savers' feast, to which Gibbs's elderly labourer referred, was organised by the local working men's friendly society and was also known as the Club Day. This occasion was often arranged for Whitsun (or Whitsunday), the seventh Sunday after Easter, known as Pentecost in the Christian calendar. Whitsun was also the traditional time for many parish feasts and parades by churches or chapels. Both types of celebration involved a sumptuous meal, often paid for by the local landowner, as well as games, music and dancing.

Getting in the harvest safely is vital for the agricultural community as its success ensures continued employment for the farmer and all his workers, as well as food for the animals over the winter. Joshua Lamb, who was a farmer in the last quarter of the nineteenth century, recalled the traditional Harvest Home celebrations in *Leslie Baily's BBC Scrapbooks*: 'Extra beer was taken to the field before the last load was picked up. From the top of the waggon the words "Up, up, up, up, harvest home!" were shouted again and again, between liberal potations from the bottle. Afterwards, all the farm hands would sit down to supper, with plum pudding, and rounds of beef, accompanied with songs and stories'.

Every village had its annual feast, which the whole community planned ahead for and looked forward to during the year. This was the time that villagers enjoyed the most, according to Pamela Horn in *Labouring Life in the Victorian Countryside*: 'On the morning of the great day stalls would be set up in the main street, displaying every kind of delicacy for sale – sausages, gingerbreads, oranges, cakes and sweets. Swingboats and roundabouts...would provide the entertainment, along with Aunt Sallies, visiting clowns and perhaps a dancing booth'. An Aunt Sally is a traditional fairground game, which involves throwing sticks at the figurine of an old woman's head to dislodge the pipe in her mouth.

Walter Rose writes about late Victorian Haddenham in Buckinghamshire in *The Village Carpenter*. He remembers that the annual feast was a time for reunions:

'No institution was more popular, or more deeply rooted in village sentiment, than our annual Feast, which fell on the first Sunday after the nineteenth of September and was always celebrated on the following day...the village always honoured the Feast with a zest that it brought to no other event...the ancient celebration was...a literal feast of good food and drink, with the mirth that goes with these things. It was a whole day of festivity, when, from outlying farms, lads and lasses, hired for the year, were given a day's leave and arrived early, buxom and smiling. Each cottage home was ready for them; the gleaned corn had been ground, the pie of pears had been made from its flour, and a joint of fresh meat had been cooked...

166

'I have heard of ploughmen not able to afford to lose the day's labour, who would rise extra early and be out on the fields when it was barely possible to see the furrows so that they might knock off for the Feast before noon. For the thrill of anticipation was in every heart; it seemed to all to be the violation of deep-rooted sentiment, to work on the day of the Feast.'

Another festival which agricultural workers were involved in took place at a nearby market town. This was the annual statute or 'hiring' fair, also known as a 'mop' fair, usually held in September or October. Farm servants were employed for twelve months at a time and they went to the fair to find a place for the year ahead. *The Graphic* (1888) describes the scene:

'There they stand in the market-place waiting for some farmer or squire to appear who questions them as to their qualifications, last place, &c. and, if satisfactory, gives them a shilling in proof of the hiring, tells them where and when to come, and the man is then free for the rest of the day. He in the first place purchases some streamers of red, white and blue ribbon, which he pins in his hat to show that he has a new master, and then merrily devotes himself to the shows, roundabouts, and all the fun of the fair. There also may be seen all the female servants, dairy maids, &c. standing in a demure row on the pavement waiting to be hired.'

The market towns also hold trading fairs during the year which are important to the farming community. The great trading fairs such as the annual Sheep Fair in Boston, Lincolnshire 'were on a much grander scale than the weekly markets and they attracted stallholders and pedlars from all around,' comments David Souden in *The Victorian Village*. He argues that 'in the face of competition from regular markets and the shops that were springing up in villages as well as in the towns... people no longer needed to stock up with goods such as cloth or sugar once or twice a year'. The ancient fairs evolve into funfairs like the famous Goose Fair at Nottingham or the Michaelmas Fair at Abingdon.

THE PUBLIC HOUSE

In working-class districts and rural areas, the public house is the hub of the community. This is where the men spend what little leisure time they have. In *Lark Rise to Candleford*, Flora Thompson describes the public house in her childhood hamlet of Juniper Hill as 'its own social centre':

> 'There the adult male population gathered every evening, to sip its half-pints, drop by drop, to make them last, and to discuss local events, wrangle over politics or farming methods, or to sing a few songs... It was as much their home as their own cottages, and far more homelike than many of them, with its roaring fire, red window curtains, and well-scoured pewter...It was exclusively a men's gathering. Their wives never accompanied them; though sometimes a woman who had got her family off hand, and so had a few halfpence to spend on herself, would knock at the back door with a

bottle or jug and perhaps linger a little, herself unseen, to listen to what was going on within.'

In Bolton, there were numerous activities centred on the public house or its gardens, as noted by Pamela Horn in *Pleasures and Pastimes in Victorian Britain*. They included 'bowling, quoits, and glee clubs', as well as 'free and easies', the forerunners of music halls. There were plays, fruit and vegetable shows, sweepstake clubs, and opportunities to play cards and dominoes'. There are also darker pursuits on offer, which the English love to bet on. Public houses and beerhouses are often linked with cockfighting, dog-fighting, badger-baiting and ratting: brutal blood sports which appeal to the Victorians' taste for a gruesome spectacle. These activities are carried out illegally, since they are banned under legislation of the 1830s and 1840s, passed specifically to deal with cruelty to animals.

If you go into a public house towards the end of the nineteenth century, you'll find they also offer non-alcoholic drinks in response to the competition from cocoa rooms. 'There is hardly a window that does not show the necessity felt to cater for other wants besides drink', wrote Charles Booth in *Life and Labour of the People in London* (1886-1903):

'All sell tobacco, not a few sell tea. 'Bovril' (a well-advertised novelty) is to be had everywhere. Hot luncheons are offered, or a mid-day joint; or 'sausages and mashed' are suggested to the hungry passer-by; at all events there will be sandwiches, biscuits, and bread and cheese. Early coffee is frequently provided, and temperance

drinks too have now a recognised place. Ginger beer is sold everywhere, and not infrequently kept on draught. These things are new, and though trifles in themselves, they serve as straws to show the way of the wind. The public-houses also connect themselves with benefit clubs, charitable concerts, and 'friendly draws'.'

CHURCH- AND CHAPEL-GOING

Although religion plays a large part in the lives of many Victorians, they are not all devoutly religious. On Sunday 30 March 1851, a unique official census is taken of attendance at all places of worship in England and Wales. This reveals that of the country's 18 million inhabitants, over seven million attended public worship that day. After making allowances for young children, invalids, the elderly and those who were at work on Sundays (totalling about 30 per cent of the population), 'it was estimated that about 60 per cent of possible worshippers attended, and 40 per cent did not', according to J. F. C. Harrison in *Early Victorian Britain*. The results are flawed because of the allowances made, but it gives a rough picture of attendees on the day.

In rural areas and small towns, the attendance is higher than in towns with a population of more than 10,000. The census also shows that in villages and country towns, the Church of England has the largest following, while the Nonconformists, such as Methodists and Baptists, are more popular in manufacturing districts. Horace Mann, the author of the report on the census, wrote: 'In cities and large towns, it is observable how absolutely insignificant a portion of the congregations is composed of artisans'. This is despite the fact they attended Sunday school in their youth, but as adults they 'soon become as utter strangers to religious ordinances as the people of a heathen country'.

While many of the working classes are regular churchgoers, middle-class observers frequently report that the Sabbath is not kept as it should be. For those who are devoutly religious, Sunday is spent in quiet pursuits such as Bible study, in-between going to church, often in the morning and the evening. This keeping of the Sabbath extends to children, who are expected to play no games and make little noise. 'We might never knit or sew or play at cards at all on Sunday, not even Beggar-my-neighbour', writes Gwen Raverat of her 1890s childhood. 'And when we went out to play tennis, we used to make our rackets into brown-paper parcels, to avoid giving offence to the people in the street!' She adds: 'There were many things we might not do, not because they were wrong in themselves, but "because of the maids". Activities on Sundays were restricted by Gwen's parents, purely to set an example to the working-class servants.

The Saturday evening ritual in the late nineteenth century was recalled by a contributor to Pat Barr's *I Remember*:

> 'clean underwear was always laid out with our Sunday clothes. I hated this night, firstly because I had to sew a clean tucker on my frock and secondly because my hair was painfully screwed in rags in order to have curls for Sunday church. We walked to church as a family, my

Father in a frock-coat with a pique liner to his waistcoat and a top hat, escorting my Mother on his arm.

'She always wore either a boa or a fur necklet. Her gigantic floral hat would be skewered on with large ornamental hat pins and anchored with a veil. Summer and winter a sunshade or an umbrella was hooked on her arm, but neither was of a size to be of the slightest protection to her hat. We children walked in front, my elder brother on the pavement edge in his Eton suit and straw boater tipped over his nose, with little brother between us. All the family wore kid gloves except me. Mine were silk and when I moved my fingers they squeaked delightfully.'

THE CULT OF MOURNING

When a family member died in Victorian England, propriety reared its head again for the upper and middle classes. Etiquette meant that the whole household, including children and the servants, had to go into mourning, and every kind of relative was mourned, even non-blood relations and connections.

Family mourning was always more prolonged than Court or national mourning 'and widows had the worst of it. Two years of black crape was considered seemly', comments Alison Adburgham in *Shops and Shopping*. She adds that 'black-edged writing paper went into black-edged envelopes sealed with black wax' and 'glovers did particularly well through the custom of presenting a pair of black kid gloves to all guests attending the funeral'.

The cult of mourning is big business for the large stores and warehouses which spring up to cater specifically for this niche market. Most drapers also have mourning departments. William Aldous was a fund-holder who lived and worked in London. In January 1863, his brother's wife died, aged around 79. On 9 January, he recorded in his diary:

'I had appointed to go to the Cemetery at Willesden at 12. M.Y. [his sister Mary Young] came in Car with Jas. A. [his brother]. We rode to cemetery met Mr France the Undertaker there by appt. We selected a piece of Ground at the back of my Grave to be placed the remains of the late Mrs Aldous to be interred on Tuesday next at 10 o'clock'.

Later that day:

'Caro [his wife's sister] rode with M.Y. to Allison's to buy mourning silks...They had selected Silks. I went with them to the Mantle Room we selected a handsome blk Velvet Cloak for So [Sophia, his second wife] 8.18.6. she pd for it I paid for Silks 11.11.9.'

As William's wife, Sophia would have worn mourning for her dead sister-in-law for between four and six months. When William himself died the following year, Sophia's mourning as a widow would have been far more severe at one year and one month for the 'first' or 'deep' mourning. (*Diary of William Aldous 1862-1864 MS 133/1, reproduced with permission of Cadbury Research Library: Special Collections, University of Birmingham*).

In this period, a widow's 'weeds' would have consisted

of 'bombazine covered with crape, a widow's cap, lawn cuffs and collars'. This was followed by six months of 'second' mourning in which less crape was worn, and a further six months of 'ordinary' mourning, according to Judith Flanders in *The Victorian House*. No crape was worn during this time, and silk or wool replaced the bombazine. It was permissible to wear jet jewellery and ribbons in the last three months of 'ordinary' mourning. Even after this long period of mourning, a respectable widow was still expected to wear half-mourning for a further six months, and permitted colours including grey, lavender, mauve and black and grey.

You'll notice that most mourning wear is worn by women but from the mid-nineteenth century onwards, men mourn close family by wearing a hatband and a black suit, for half the period of mourning prescribed for women. Widowers are the only exception, and their mourning is worn for three months. Degrees of mourning and the etiquette which goes with it are complex, even for the Victorians. Magazines regularly publish articles on the subject for their middle-class readers or respond to their specific queries. At all costs, the middle classes want to be seen to be respectable. Of course, for the working classes, special clothes for mourning are out of the question, so a black trimming on a hat might be all they can offer as a gesture of respect for their dead relative. Mourning etiquette does not therefore apply to them.

The custom of women attending funerals is also complicated, although it is generally accepted that those from the upper classes and the working classes could, and did. Whether women attended or not appears to have differed from family to family; although she famously mourned him for decades, Queen Victoria did not go to the funeral of her own husband.

CHILDBIRTH AND CHRISTENINGS

The arrival of a new baby into a Victorian family was also full of tradition. When labour began, the mother was 'confined' to her room. Dearman and Emily Birchall's third child was born in 1878. As a landowner and country gentleman, Dearman could afford the best medical attendance for his wife. On 2 October, he wrote in his diary:

> '12.35 this morning Emily was safely confined of a daughter. Mr Graves came at 11.30 p.m. He gave her chloroform at once and it was soon over. The after pains were very severe and she had considerable haemorrhage which made her excessively faint. Graves gave her two or three glasses of brandy and a sleeping draught. She was so nervous with the faintness that he stayed all night. Little girl (Violet) weighs 8 lbs.'

Contrast this with the experience of most working-class women who had little or no access to pain relief or medical help, other than a midwife. Hannah Mitchell's husband was a shop assistant in Bolton, earning 25 shillings a week when she had her first child in the 1890s. J. F. C. Harrison quotes from her autobiography, *The Hard Way Up*:

> 'I feared the ordeal, but tried to keep my fears to myself... At last my own time came...I hoped for a good night's

rest, but I scarcely had retired before my labour began. My baby was not born until the following evening, after twenty-four hours of intense suffering which an ignorant attendant did little to alleviate, assuring me at intervals that I should be much worse yet. At last, a kindly neighbour...sent my husband for the doctor, charging him to insist on immediate attendance, and bustled me into bed. But my strength was gone, and I could do no more to help myself, so my baby was brought into the world with instruments, and without an anaesthetic.'

The main danger of childbirth was puerperal fever (also known as 'childbed' fever), a bacterial infection which could set in from the third or tenth day. It was caused by the poor hygiene of the medical attendants or by the unhygienic implements used during the birth.

For this reason, it was recommended that mothers should remain in bed for ten days after the birth and only get up on a sofa for the next four or five days. It was important to take the mother's temperature, morning and night, and to call a doctor if it reached over 100° F; a high temperature was a warning of the onset of fever.

According to tradition, it was also vital that the mother was not seen by anyone outside the family before she had been 'churched'. This was the cleansing ceremony carried out on her first visit to church about three weeks after the birth, and this could not be done until the danger of fever or other complications had passed.

'Even the rentman or any other callers who had not been invited to the house had to be avoided', wrote Albert Goodwin, quoted in John Burnett's *Destiny*

Obscure. 'This was rigidly carried out and anyone who overstepped the bounds was a subject of scandalous gossip among the neighbours. The baby could be shown and praised (especially when the Father was around and there was something to 'wet the baby's head') but the mother had to suffer the pangs of isolation'.

The christening of a child usually took place between four and six weeks after its birth, after the mother had been 'churched'. This custom was adhered to, even if the parents did not regularly attend church or chapel. The exception was when the baby was not expected to live and was then baptised at home by the local vicar, priest or minister. The choice of godparents was an important one because in Victorian England, the chance of both parents dying before their child became of age was relatively high; one of the godparents would become the orphan's guardian in the legal and physical sense of the word.

Exquisitely embroidered white christening gowns were handed down the generations for the baby to wear on the special day, even in working-class homes. After the christening, family and friends congregated at the parents' home and might be offered cake; for a first-born, traditionally, this was from the top tier of the parents' wedding cake. Sterling silver rattles, egg cups, tankards and spoons were popular christening gifts, then as now, particularly for the middle classes and the wealthy, since they were tangible items of monetary value. As childbirth was universal, the old traditions held fast whether the parents lived in a large town or a rural village. In the countryside, customs specific to a particular area might also be practised.

Although age-old traditions are upheld in rural England, fewer people live there than ever before. England becomes the world's first urbanised nation when the 1851 census reveals that more than half of the population live in towns of 20,000 people or more. By 1901, the proportion rises to three-quarters. Rural areas cannot escape the march of mechanisation and when it is introduced in farming, it changes not only the landscape, but also the soundscape.

'Up to the year 1872 there were neither reaping nor mowing machines on our farm of over 600 acres, and I remember during haytime I used to love to watch the string of mowers with their scythes following each other across a field of grass or clover, often six together', recalled Joshua Lamb, a farmer in the remote village of Sibford Ferris, Oxfordshire, quoted in *Leslie Baily's BBC Scrapbooks*. 'The thud of the flail on the barn floor, the blind horse pacing round and round attached by a pole to an old threshing machine, the patient oxen plodding before the wooden plough, the harsh cry of the corncrake and the call of the quail, these, together with many other sights and sounds of my childhood, have passed away'.

APPENDICES

TIMELINE

1837   Queen Victoria ascends the throne at the age of 18

1837   London's first railway station opens at Euston

1838   Regular steamship services between Britain and the USA begin

1838   The London to Birmingham railway line opens

1839   William Fox Talbot invents the photographic process, at the same time as the Frenchman Daguerre

1839   *Bradshaw's Railway Companion*, the first national railway timetable, is published

1840   Queen Victoria marries Prince Albert of Saxe-Coburg-Gotha

1840   The first adhesive postage stamps are introduced: the Penny Black and the Twopence Blue

1841   Thomas Cook organises his first railway excursion from Leicester to Loughborough; the passengers are 540 campaigners for temperance attending a rally

1842 The Mines and Collieries Act prohibits women and girls from working underground, as well as boys under ten years old

1842 Queen Victoria takes her first journey by train from Slough to Paddington

1844 The first co-operative shop is opened by the Rochdale Pioneers Society in Rochdale

1847 Chloroform is used as an anaesthetic for the first time by Dr James Simpson

1847 The Factory Act (Ten Hour Act) limits the work-day to ten hours for women and children under 18 employed in textile mills

1848 There is a global cholera pandemic, killing 21,000 in England

1848 W. H. Smith opens his first railway bookstall at Euston Station, London

1848 Under the Public Health Act, every new house must have a water closet, privy or ash pit

1851 The Great Exhibition at the Crystal Palace in Hyde Park is open between May and October

1853 Queen Victoria uses chloroform during the birth of her seventh child, Leopold

1853 There is another cholera epidemic, which kills 15,000 people in England

1855 Florence Nightingale introduces nursing reforms in the Crimean War

1857 Divorce courts are established under the Matrimonial Causes Act

1860 The first tramway opens at Birkenhead

1861 Prince Albert dies of typhoid and Queen Victoria goes into mourning

1862 The cotton famine has disastrous effects for the Lancashire mill workers; by November, three-fifths are unemployed

1863 The first section of the London Underground, the Metropolitan Railway Line, is opened to passengers

1865 Joseph Lister applies carbolic acid to the wounds of a patient to create antiseptic conditions

1866 The fourth cholera epidemic breaks out; this time, it kills 6,000 people

1867 Thomas Barnardo sets up his first Ragged School for poor children in London's East End

1867 Male householders paying rates and men who pay rent of at least £10 a year become eligible to vote under the Reform Act

1867 The velocipede or 'bone-shaker' bicycle is introduced

1868 The last public execution takes place outside Newgate Prison: Michael Barrett killed 12 people and injured more than 50 others with a bomb at Clerkenwell, an act of terrorism for the Fenian cause

1870 The 'ordinary' or 'high wheel' bicycle, known as a penny farthing, is introduced

1870 The Elementary Education Act provides free school places for all children aged between five and 12 years

1870 Postcards are introduced and can be posted for a halfpenny

1871 Bank Holidays Act: Whit Monday becomes the country's first Bank Holiday

1872 The Midland Railway is the first to carry third-class passengers on all its trains

1872 The first English FA Cup Final takes place at the Oval: Wanderers beat the Royal Engineers; the score is 1-0

1873 The first trains to provide sleeping cars are run by the North British Railway from Glasgow and Edinburgh through to London

1874 The Factory Act raises the minimum working age of children to ten years

1875 The Public Health Act requires every local authority to appoint a Medical Officer of Health, as well as local sanitary inspectors

1876 Alexander Graham Bell invents the telephone

1877 The first shipment of frozen meat reaches Britain from Argentina

1877 The first cricket Test Match takes place in Melbourne – Australia beat England

1877 The first men's singles tennis final is played at Wimbledon – Spencer Gore wins

1877 Queen Victoria is proclaimed Empress of India

1878 The safety bicycle is invented

1878 Under the Factory and Workshop Act, no child under ten can be employed in any trade and 10 to 14 year olds can only work half-days

1878 The first reliable filament electric lamp is demonstrated by Joseph Swan

1879 The first illuminations at Blackpool are staged

1879 The Great Northern Railway provides the first restaurant car on a British train on the route between King's Cross and Leeds

1880 The Education Act makes attending school compulsory for children up to ten years old

1880 Greenwich Mean Time applies to the whole country for the first time

1884 The Franchise Act entitles many more adult males to vote, but 40 per cent are still excluded, as are women

1885 John Kemp Starley invents the first commercially successful safety bicycle, called the Rover

1885 The first modern cremation is carried out at Woking Crematorium; the deceased was Jeanette Pickersgill, the wife of artist Henry William Pickersgill

1887 Queen Victoria's Golden Jubilee

1888   John Boyd Dunlop patents the pneumatic tyre, which makes cycling more comfortable

1888   Jack the Ripper murders at least five women in Whitechapel, East London

1890   Elementary education in junior schools is made free for the first time

1894   Michael Marks goes into partnership with Tom Spencer to form the first branch of Marks & Spencer (Penny Bazaars)

1897   Queen Victoria's Diamond Jubilee

1899   The Boer War begins, more correctly known as the Second Boer War

1901   Queen Victoria dies on 22 January aged 81; she has reigned for 63 years

CURRENCY AND COINAGE

When you visit any foreign country, it's always useful to acquaint yourself with the currency and coinage beforehand; the same would be true of Victorian England.

Pre-decimal coinage was then in place, so money was divided into pounds (£), shillings (s) and pence (d). For example, five pounds three shillings and four pence would be written as £5 3s 4d. In shops, money would also be written in an abbreviated form. Three shillings and four pence can be shortened to: 3/4

One farthing is worth a quarter of one penny (¼d)

One halfpenny is worth half of one penny (½d)

One threepenny (a silver coin) is worth three pennies (3d)

One groat is worth four pennies (4d)

One sixpence (also called a 'tanner') is worth six pennies (6d)

One shilling (1s or 1/-) is worth twelve pence (12d)

One florin is worth two shillings (2s)

Half a crown is worth two shillings sixpence (2s 6d)

One crown is worth five shillings (5s)

One half sovereign is worth ten shillings (10s)

One sovereign (or one pound) is worth 20 shillings (20/-)

One guinea is worth 21 shillings (£1 1s)

It's highly unlikely that you will come into contact with any paper money, since notes are reserved for higher denominations than a guinea.

COSTS OF ACCOMMODATION

Black's Picturesque Tourist and Road and Railway Guide Book Through England and Wales (1850) provides a very helpful scale of charges travellers could expect to pay. The lower charges are for the inns in smaller towns and in villages, where costs might be even more moderate. The higher charges were made by the highest class hotels in the principal cities:

	Country	Towns/cities
Breakfast	1s 6d to 2s	2s to 8s
Dinner	2s to 3s	3s to 4s
Tea	1s 6d to 2s	2s to 3s
Supper	1s 6d to 2s	(According to what is ordered)
Port or sherry, per bottle	5s to 6s	6s
Porter or ale, per bottle	6d to 1s	1s
Brandy, per gill	1s 6d	2s
Whisky, per gill	9d	1s
Bed	1s 6d to 3s	3s 6d to 4s

By 1870, the separate cost of attendance increases to between 1s and 1s 6d in the cheapest places and 2s to 5s in more upmarket hotels. In a small village inn, a private room costs between 2s and 5s, while in the high-class hotel, it is 5s to 10s.

Wages and Salaries

Here are some sample salaries and weekly wages for various occupations in the last quarter of the nineteenth century. The amounts for those in domestic service are comparatively low, but food and lodging was provided by the employer.

A cashier in a solicitor's office	£150 per annum
A Poor Law officer in London	£90 per annum

An office clerk	£80 per annum
A butler	£58 6s per annum
A housekeeper	£52 2s per annum
A footman	£26 7s per annum
A lady's maid	£24 7s per annum
A parlourmaid	£20 6s per annum
A cook	£20 2s per annum
A housemaid	£16 2s per annum
A railway foreman in Kent	25s 10d per week (average)
A coffee-stall keeper	£1 per week (average)
A general labourer	£1 per week (average)
A female copying-clerk (London)	£1 per week (average)
A Cornish fisherman	10s 10d per week (average)

Sources: Board of Trade surveys from Miss Collet's *Report* (1894-98); *Family Budgets*, 1891-94; Picard, Liza, *Victorian London: The Life of a City 1840–1870* (Weidenfeld & Nicolson, 2005).

WHAT YOU COULD BUY WITH...

One half-penny:
Send a postcard
A sheath (condom)
Half a mug of coffee, tea or cocoa at a coffee stall

One penny:
Send a letter by post
A popular daily newspaper such as *The Daily Graphic*
or *The Daily News*
The weekly fee for a child to attend a board school
Admission to a plunge bath at a public baths
A pint of common beer
Three Yarmouth bloaters (herring)
Three oysters
A bunch of turnips
Twenty hot chestnuts
Admission to a 'penny gaff'
A packet of Bayly's insect killer
Any item in the Marks & Spencer's 'Penny Bazaars'

Twopence:
A pint of milk
Admission to a warm private bath at a public baths
A seat in a gallery at the theatre

Threepence:
The Times or the *Morning Post* newspaper
The average fare to travel by omnibus

Fourpence:
The second-class fare on the Metropolitan Railway
from Moorgate to Praed Street (first-class was 6d and
third-class, 3d)

Fivepence:
A man's collar
An ounce of tobacco

Sixpence:
One cigar

Soap (1½ lbs)
Williams' 'Jersey Cream' shaving soap
A tin of Keating's powder which destroys bugs, fleas,
moths and beetles

Seven pence:
Canary and domestic wax candles (per lb)

Eight pence:
A man's pair of cuffs
A loaf of bread (about 4 lbs)
Tinned Australian mutton (per lb)

Tenpence:
A pair of socks
Sugar (4 lbs)
Parlour or drawing room wax candles (per lb)

One shilling:
Send a telegram (plus 3d for every additional
five words)
Cocoa (per lb)
A toothbrush
A Za-zah voice flute
The fare for a cab in London for a journey of up to two
miles (6d extra for each additional or part of a mile)
Admission to the Great Exhibition on the cheapest day of
the week
Admission to London's Cremorne Gardens

One shilling twopence:
A box of Barton's Exterminator for killing rats and mice

One shilling threepence:
Coal (1 cwt)

One shilling sixpence:
Coffee (per lb)
Kerosene oil (per gallon)
A pair of black silk hose

Two shillings:
Tea (per lb)

Two shillings sixpence:
A man's under-vest
A man's hat
A bottle of Floriline for the teeth and breath, 'the best liquid dentrifice in the world'

Three shillings:
A man's flannel shirt

Three shillings sixpence:
A small bottle of Rowland's Macassar Oil
A dozen pints of Bass Pale Ale
Finest French Colza oil, suitable for all lamps (per gallon)

Three shillings ninepence:
A dozen ladies' white cambric hem-stitched pocket handkerchiefs
The 'United Service' trousers stretcher (to avoid baggy knees)

Four shillings:
A seat in the upper circle at a theatre
A bottle of Mariani wine, said to quickly restore health, strength, energy and vitality

Four shillings elevenpence:
A lady's Y & N diagonal seam corset (starting price, per pair)

Five shillings:
The weekly rent for a three-room flat, built by Angela
Burdett-Coutts for the industrious poor

Five shillings sixpence:
A 'Busy Bee' sewing machine
A black-handled Kropp razor, which never needs
grinding
A good silk top hat

Six shillings:
Cost of repairing boots

Six shillings sixpence:
A crinoline

Six shillings elevenpence:
A boy's Royal Navy suit consisting of blue serge
blouse with badge on arm and knickerbockers, flannel
singlet, lanyard and whistle (starting price)

Seven shillings sixpence:
An umbrella
A man's silk hat

Ten shillings sixpence (half a guinea):
A pair of men's boots
A seat in the stalls at a theatre
A Cleveland camera and lens in mahogany
Six pairs of ladies' Paris-made suede gloves
A 'Pelican' fountain pen with a shut-off valve
A Christmas hamper containing one good hen turkey,
Cambridge sausages and Devonshire butter (1lb)
A calisthenics lesson
The cost of two fillings from a fashionable dentist

Ten shillings ninepence:
A tin travelling trunk with two leather straps

Fifteen shillings:
A 4ft 6 inch black and brass French bedstead
A first-class excursion train ticket from York to London

Sixteen shillings:
A pair of ladies' kid elastic boots

Seventeen shillings sixpence:
A pair of Dollond's aluminium opera glasses

Seventeen shillings ninepence:
A portmanteau

Eighteen shillings:
A Multiphone musical box, complete with five barrels

One pound (or twenty shillings):
A set of twelve *carte de visite* portrait photographs

One pound 1 shilling (a guinea or twenty-one shillings):
A Harness' Electropathic Belt from The Medical Battery Company, said to cure rheumatism, indigestion and all nervous affections
A boy's knickerbocker suit

One pound fifteen shillings:
A man's overcoat

Two pounds:
A man's weekday suit

Two pounds eight shillings:
A first-class rail and steam return ticket to Paris (third-class was £1 4s)

Two pounds ten shillings:
A man's Sunday suit

Two pounds twelve shillings sixpence:
A lady's fur-lined cashmere cloak (starting price)

Two pounds fifteen shillings:
A lady's ball dress

Sources: *The Times; The Illustrated London News; The Daily Graphic; Black & White;* Langbridge, R. H. (ed.), *Life In The 1870s As Seen Through Advertisements In* The Times (Times Books, 1974); Picard, Liza, *Victorian London: The Life of a City 1840-1870* (Weidenfeld & Nicolson, 2005). Hill, Miranda, 'Life on Thirty Shillings a Week' in *The Nineteenth Century* (March 1888); Leyard, George Somes, 'How to Live on £700 a Year' in *The Nineteenth Century* (February 1888); Roberts, W., 'Life on a Guinea a Week' in *The Nineteenth Century* (March 1888) [extracts of this article appear on The Victorian Web, courtesy of Richard Patterson].

[N.B. Then, as now, prices vary depending upon which type of shop goods are bought from]

THE COST OF LIVING

The following are budgets suggested to readers of the *Cornhill Magazine* in 1901.

'How To Live On Thirty Shillings A Week'

	£	s	d
Rent		7	0
Meat and fish		5	5
Bread and flour		2	1½
Grocery		1	8
Cheese, butter, bacon and eggs		1	11
Greengrocery		1	3
Firing		2	0
Oil and sundries		1	7½
Allowance for clothes		2	0
Club and insurance		1	0
Beer and tobacco		2	9
Balance in hand for contingencies, petty cash etc.		1	3
	£1	10	0

(Source: Arthur Morrison, *Cornhill Magazine*, April 1901)

'How To Live On A Hundred And Fifty A Year'

	£	s	d
Rent (£26), rates and taxes (£5 3s 5d)	31	3	5
Railway travelling	7	0	0
Life insurance and benefit club	4	8	3
Newspapers, books, etc.	4	10	0
Gas, coal, coke, oil, wood, matches	9	17	0
Summer holiday	5	0	0
Tobacco	2	5	0
Birthday and Christmas presents	1	10	0
Stamps and stationery		12	0
Food	47	9	0
House expenses	5	4	0
Boots	6	0	0
Tailor	6	0	0
Dress for wife and children	13	0	0
Balance to cover doctor, chemist, charities, &c.	6	1	4
	£150	0	0

(Source: G. S. Layard, *Cornhill Magazine*, May 1901)

'How To Live On Eight Hundred A Year'

	£	s	d
Rent, rates and taxes	130	0	0
Housekeeping	208	0	0
Servants' wages	38	0	0
Husband's allowance	70	0	0
Wife's allowance	70	0	0
Repairs	50	0	0
Holidays	50	0	0
Doctor	30	0	0
Wine	20	0	0
Tobacco	10	0	0
Coal	12	0	0
Gas	9	0	0
Stationery	5	0	0
Postage, &c.	13	0	0
Entertaining, &c.	35	0	0
	£750	0	0

(Source: G. Colmore, *Cornhill Magazine*, June 1901)

'How To Live On Eighteen Hundred A Year'

	£	s	d
Rent, rates and taxes	360	0	0
Housekeeping, including living, washing and lighting	550	0	0
Repairs, insurance, cleaning, painting, etc.	100	0	0
Coal	60	0	0
Dress (man and woman)	200	0	0
Wages, including beer, and 4 servants	130	0	0
Wine	60	0	0
Stamps, newspapers, stationery, etc.	30	0	0
Doctors, dentists, accidents, journeys	100	0	0
New house linen	20	0	0
Charities	40	0	0
	£1650	0	0

(Source: Mrs Earle, *Cornhill Magazine*, July 1901)

BIBLIOGRAPHY

An Old Stager, *Hints to Railway Travellers and Country Visitors to London* (Bradbury & Evans, 1852)

Baily, Leslie, *Leslie Baily's BBC Scrapbooks Volume 1: 1896-1914* (George Allen & Unwin, 1966)

Barr, Pat (ed.), *I Remember: An Arrangement for Many Voices* (Macmillan, 1970)

Bartlett, David W., *What I Saw in London, or Men and Things in the Great Metropolis* (1853)

Batts, John Stuart, *British Manuscript Diaries of the Nineteenth Century* (Centaur Press, 1976)

Beadle, Charles, *Reminiscences of a Victorian* (originally published 1924)

Beeton, Mrs Isabella, *The Book of Household Management* (S O Beeton Publishing, 1861)

Bennett, Alfred Rosling, *London and Londoners in the 1850s and 1860s* (Victorian London Ebooks, originally published 1924)

Best, Geoffrey, *Mid-Victorian Britain 1851-1875* (Fontana Press, 1979)

Black's Guide to England and Wales (Adam and Charles Black, 1870)

Black's Picturesque Tourist and Road and Railway Guide Book Through England and Wales (Adam and Charles Black, 1850)

Booth, Charles, *Life and Labour of the People of London* (1886-1903)

Bradshaw's Handbook for Tourists (1863)

Briggs, Asa, *Victorian Cities* (Penguin Books, 1968)

Burnett, John (ed.), *Destiny Obscure: Autobiographies of Childhood, Education and Family from the 1820s to the 1920s* (Allen Lane, 1982)

Burnett, John (ed.), *Useful Toil: Autobiographies of Working People from the 1820s to the 1920s* (Routledge, 1994)

Burton, Elizabeth, *The Early Victorians at Home* (Arrow Books, 1974)

Cassell's Family Magazine (1885)

Cassell's Handbook of Etiquette: Being a Complete Guide to the Usages of Polite Society (Cassell, Petter and Gallpin, 1860)

Chancellor, Valerie E. (ed.), *Master & Artisan in Victorian England: The Diary of William Andrews and the Autobiography of Joseph Gutteridge* (Augustus M. Kelley, 1969)

Colman, Henry, *European Life and Manners in Familiar Letters to Friends* (1850)

Contrasts in a Victorian City: Birmingham (Birmingham City Council, 1995)

Cook, Chris, *Britain in the Nineteenth Century 1815-1914* (Longman, 1999)

Cooper, Margaret (ed.), *A Victorian Lady's Diary 1838-1842, Elizabeth Nutt Harwood of Beeston* (Nottinghamshire County Council, 2005)

Cornish's Stranger's Guide through Birmingham (Cornish Brothers, 1858)

Cumming, Valerie, Cunnington, C. W. and Cunnington, P. E., *The Dictionary of Fashion History* (Berg, 2010)

Davidson, Lillias Campbell, *Hints to Lady Travellers: At Home and Abroad* (Iliffe & Son, 1889)

Davies, Margaret Llewelyn (ed.), *Life As We Have Known It By Co-operative Working Women* (Virago Press, 1977)

Engels, Friedrich, *The Condition of the Working-Class in England in 1844* (1892)

Flanders, Judith, *The Victorian City: Everyday Life in Dickens' London* (Atlantic Books, 2012)

Flanders, Judith, *The Victorian House: Domestic Life from Childbirth to Deathbed* (Harper Collins, 2003)

Gard, Robin, *The Observant Traveller: Diaries of Travel in England, Wales and Scotland in the County Record Offices of England and Wales* (HMSO, 1989)

Gavin, Hector, *Sanitary Ramblings, Being Sketches and Illustrations of Bethnal Green* (John Churchill, 1848)

Gibbs, J. Arthur, *A Cotswold Village, or Country Life and Pursuits in Gloucestershire* (J. Murray, 1898)

Granville, Augustus Bozzi, *The Spas of England and Principal Sea-Bathing Places* (Henry Colburn, 1841)

Halliday, Stephen, *The Great Filth: The War Against Disease in Victorian England* (Sutton Publishing, 2007)

Hannavy, John, *The English Seaside in Victorian and Edwardian Times* (Shire Publications, 2008)

Harrison, J. F. C., *Early Victorian Britain 1832-1851* (Fontana Press, 1988)

Harrison, J. F. C., *Late Victorian Britain 1875-1901* (Fontana Press, 1990)

Hawthorne, Nathaniel, *Passages from the English Note-Books* (James R. Osgood and Company, 1871)

Heath, Richard, *The English Peasant* (1893)

Hibbert, Christopher, *The Illustrated London News Social History of Victorian Britain* (Angus & Robertson, 1975)

Hill, Miranda, 'Life on Thirty Shillings a Week' in *The Nineteenth Century* (March 1888)

Hollingshead, John, *Odd Journeys In and Out of London* (Groombridge & Sons, 1860)

Hollingshead, John, *Ways of Life* (Groombridge & Sons, 1861)

Horn, Pamela, *Labouring Life in the Victorian Countryside* (Alan Sutton Publishing, 1987)

Horn, Pamela, *Pleasures and Pastimes in Victorian Britain* (Sutton Publishing, 1999)

Hudson, Derek (ed.), *Munby, Man of Two Worlds: The Life and Diaries of Arthur F. Munby 1828-1910* (John Murray, 1972)

Hughes, M. V., *A London Child of the 1870s* (Oxford University Press, 1934)

Hughes, M. V., *A London Girl of the 1880s* (Oxford University Press, 1946)

Hughes, M. V., *A London Home in the 1890s* (Oxford University Press, 1946)

Kelsall, Helen and Keith (ed.), *Diary of a Victorian Miss on Holiday* (The Hallamshire Press, 1992)

Jackson, Lee (ed.), *Daily Life in Victorian London: An Extraordinary Anthology* (Victorian London Ebooks, 2011)

Jefferies, Richard, *Hodge and His Masters* (Smith, Elder & Co., 1880)

Jefferies, Richard, *Round About a Great Estate* (Smith, Elder & Co., 1880)

Keating, Peter (ed.), *Into Unknown England 1866-1913: Selections from the Social Explorers* (Fontana, 1976)

Killick, Jane, *Talking with Past Hours: The Victorian Diary of William Fletcher of Bridgnorth* (Moonrise Press, 2009)

Kirk's Popular Guide (1889)

Knight, Charles, *Knight's Excursion Companion: Excursions from London* (Charles Knight, 1851)

Lady, A, *The Workwoman's Guide* (Simpkin, Marshall & Co., 1840)

Langbridge, R. H. (ed.), *Life in the 1870s As Seen Through Advertisements in The Times* (Times Books, 1974)

Leyard, George Somes, 'How to Live on £700 a Year' in *The Nineteenth Century* (February 1888)

Linder, Leslie (ed.), *The Journal of Beatrix Potter, 1881-1897* (Frederick Warne Publishers Ltd, 1989)

Manby Smith, Charles, *The Little World of London* (Arthur Hall, 1857)

Martineau, Harriet, *A Complete Guide to the English Lakes* (John Garnett, 1855)

Mayhew, Henry, *London Labour and the London Poor* (1861)

McKenny, Helen G., *A City Road Diary: The Record of Three Years in London* (World Methodist Historical Society, 1978)

Measom, George, *The Official Illustrated Guide to the Great Eastern Railway* (C. Griffin & Co., 1865)

Miles, Alice, *Every Girl's Duty: The Diary of a Victorian Debutante* (BCA, 1992)

Mitford, Mary Russell, *Our Village* (1832)

Mogg's Great Western Railway and Windsor, Bath and Bristol Guide (E. Mogg, 1842)

Mogg's Omnibus Guide and Metropolitan Carriage Time Table (E. Mogg, 1848)

Nicholson, Shirley, *A Victorian Household* (Sutton Publishing, 1988)

O'Rell, Max, *John Bull and His Island* (1884)

Osborne's Guide to the Grand Junction, or Birmingham, Liverpool and Manchester Railway (E. C. and W. Osborne, 1838)

Osborne's London & Birmingham Railway Guide (E. C. & W. Osborne, 1840)

Panton, Jane Ellen, *From Kitchen to Garret* (Ward & Downey, 1888)

Pardon, George Frederick, *The Popular Guide to London and its Suburbs* (Routledge, Warne and Routledge, 1852)

Paxman, Jeremy, *The Victorians: Britain Through the Paintings of the Age* (Random House, 2009)

Pearsall, Ronald, *The Worm in the Bud: The World of Victorian Sexuality* (Pimlico, 1993)

Picard, Liza, *Victorian London: The Life of a City 1840-1870* (Weidenfeld & Nicolson, 2005)

Plomer, William (ed.), *Kilvert's Diary: Selections from the Diary of the Rev. Francis Kilvert 23 August 1871-13 May 1874 Volume Two* (Jonathan Cape, 1960)

Pountney, Adelaide, *The Diary of a Victorian Lady: Scenes from her Life 1864-1865* (Excellent Press, 1998)

Quennell, Peter, *Victorian Panorama: A Survey of Life & Fashion from Contemporary Photographs* (B. T. Batsford Ltd, 1937)

Raverat, Gwen, *Period Piece: A Cambridge Childhood* (Faber & Faber, 1952)

Roberts, W., 'Life on a Guinea a Week' in *The Nineteenth Century* (March 1888)

Rose, Walter, *The Village Carpenter* (1937)

Royston Pike, E., *Human Documents of the Age of the Forsytes* (George Allen & Unwin Ltd, 1969)

Royston Pike, E., *Human Documents of the Victorian Golden Age* (George Allen & Unwin Ltd, 1967)

Sala, George Augustus, *Twice Round the Clock* (Houlston & Wright, 1859)

Sambrook, G. A. (ed.), *English Life in the Nineteenth Century* (Macmillan & Co. Ltd, 1954)

Schlesinger, Max, *Saunterings In and About London* (Nathaniel Cooke, 1853)

Sherburne, John Henry, *The Tourist's Guide, or Pencillings in England and on the Continent* (G. B. Zieber & Co., 1847)

Shonfield, Zuzanna, *The Precariously Privileged: A Professional Family in Victorian London* (Oxford University Press, 1987)

Souden, David, *The Victorian Village* (Collins & Brown, 1991)

Stamper, Joseph, *So Long Ago* (Hutchinson, 1960)

Streatfeild, Noel (ed.), *The Day Before Yesterday* (Collins, 1956)

Taine, Hippolyte, *Notes on England* (Holt & Williams, 1872)

The American Stranger's Guide to London and Liverpool at Table (Longman Green, Longman & Roberts, 1859)

The Gazetteer and Directory of Worcestershire (1873)

The History & Directory of Furness and Cartmel (P. Mannex and Co., 1882)

The Magazine of Domestic Economy (1837-1843)

The Midland Counties Railway Companion (R. Allen and E. Allen, 1840)

The Visitor's Guide to Bournemouth and Its Neighbourhood (Ackerman, 1850)

The Visitor's Guide to Malvern (H. W. Lamb)

The Watering Places of England (Society for Promoting Christian Knowledge, 1853)

Thompson, Flora, *Lark Rise to Candleford* (1945)

Verey, David (ed.), *The Diary of a Victorian Squire: Extracts from the Diaries and Letters of Dearman and Emily Birchall* (Alan Sutton Publishing, 1983)

Wells, H. G., *Experiment in Autobiography* (1934)

Wilson, A. N., *The Victorians*, (Hutchinson, 2007)

Winstanley, Michael J., *The Shopkeeper's World 1830-1914* (Manchester University Press, 1983)

Wise, Dorothy (ed.), *Diary of William Tayler, Footman 1837* (The St Marylebone Society, 1987)

Wright, Thomas, *Some Habits and Customs of the Working Classes* (Tinsley Brothers, 1867)

Original sources

Diary of John Whaley 1848 (D/AR 65), Durham County Record Office

Diary of William Aldous 1862-1864 (MS 133/1), Cadbury Research Library: Special Collections, University of Birmingham

Websites

Roberts, W., "Life on a Guinea a Week" in *The Nineteenth Century* (1888), The Victorian Web. Ed. Richard Patterson: *www.victorianweb.org/economics/wages4.html*

Sainsbury's Archive Virtual Museum: *www.sainsburys.lgfl.org.uk*

Victorian London: *www.victorianlondon.org*

Victorian Web: *www.victorianweb.org*

Index

Discover how your Victorian ancestors lived – at findmypast.co.uk

The nineteenth century was a time of massive social change in Britain. Railways sprang up, connecting people across the country; the 1834 New Poor Law consigned millions to the workhouse; women gained new legal rights; legislation opened up education to working-class children; and ordinary people were able to travel across the world. The Victorian era was also the age of administration – the census began to record families' movements, while birth, marriage and death records charted landmarks within individual lives.

Taking your family tree into the nineteenth century and beyond is a complex process, but you'll find it easier if you make full use of all available public records. The best way to do so is to search them online. At *www.findmypast.co.uk* you'll find millions of digitised records to help you discover your heritage or flesh out the stories behind your family tree.

Britain's leading family history website covers everything from the census to parish registers, occupational records to institution registers. Simple to search and with original documents available on screen in seconds, it is both the ideal starting point for researchers and a brilliant resource to help more experienced genealogists uncover new information.

- Learn how your Victorian forebears' circumstances changed between each decade in the first national census records, from 1841 to 1911.

- Were your ancestors rich or paupers? Find out whether they sought help from the state using workhouse and Poor Law records.

- New divorce laws made it easier for couples to end unhappy marriages in the mid-nineteenth century. Find out the truth in detailed divorce case files.

- Thousands of Britons emigrated during the nineteenth century. Track their journeys through ship passenger records.

- Did your ancestor fight during the Boer War? Extensive military records enable you to learn more about soldiers and sailors who fought for Queen Victoria.

Read all about them!

If your ancestor hit the headlines during the nineteenth century, then you can easily access scans of original news reports through a simple online search. Findmypast.co.uk is working with the British Library to digitise its collection of local British newspapers and already has over 6.5 million pages from 1710 to 1963 online. You can search these by using the names of ancestors, dates, locations and key words. Search the newspapers at *www.findmypast.co.uk/search/newspapers*

Find out more about available records and pricing at *www.findmypast.co.uk*